The man with

K
DOSC

Thames & Hudson

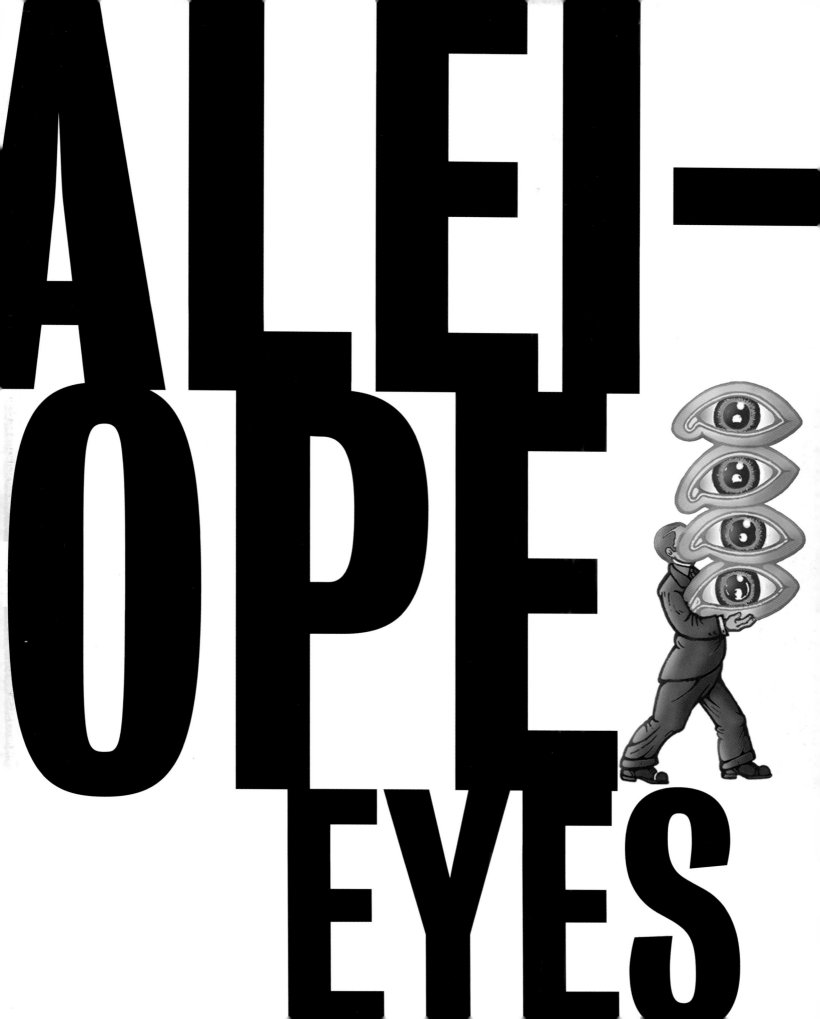

by Alan

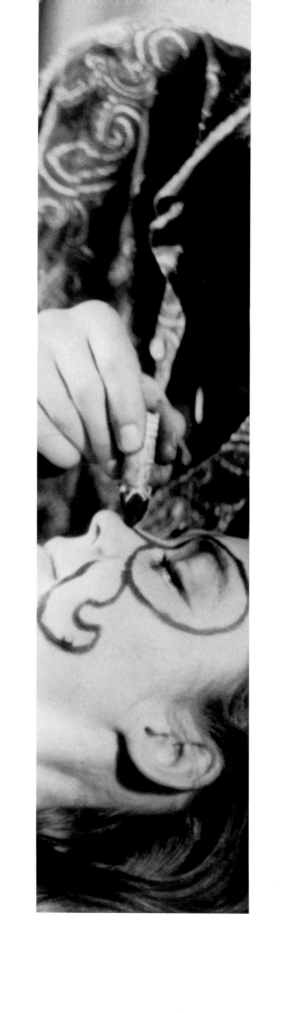

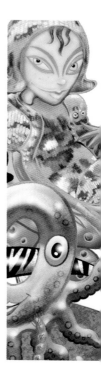

including
New Society 18,

Sunday Times 21,

Penguin Books 30,

Chelsea Girls 76,

Ann in the Moon 83,

The Butterfly Ball 94,

The Peacock Party 122,

Shadow Racing Car 130,

The Lion's Cavalcade 132,

Mr Love Pants 170,
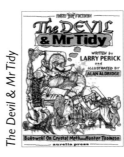
The Devil & Mr Tidy 179,

The Beatles Reprised 180,

Bozo's 192,

The Boy with the Broken Heart 204,

Solange 206,

The Beatles 48,

The Who 68,

Cream 74,

Elton John 102,

The Ship's Cat 116,

Heineken 120,

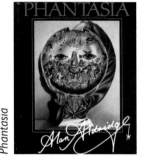
Phantasia 142,

The Gnole 152,

House of Blues 160,

The Mother Goose Mystery 184,

Tears for Fears 188,

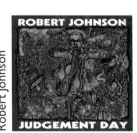
Robert Johnson 190,

Incubus 216,

Kenzo 224,

Index & acknowledgments 236

Above Alan Aldridge and Sir Elton John,
Los Angeles, March 2008.

Opposite *The Heart is a Lonely Hunter*,
Kilimanjaro magazine, 2007.

'I can't remember whose idea it was to ask Alan to work on the *Captain Fantastic* album. Whoever it was I am so grateful to them. For a start I didn't think we'd get him – and when we did he delivered a visual package beyond my wildest dreams. Never have I been so pleased with the artwork for an album – and I do mean Art. Alan delivered something that still looks amazing today – a true test of any artist. His amazing mind plus his incredible visual skills gave us what we wanted and more. Plus, he's an extremely nice chap. I am forever grateful to him.'

Sir Elton John

INTRODUCTION

'Come to the edge,' he said.
I said, 'I am afraid!'
'Come to the edge,' he said.
I did.
He pushed me ...
And I flew.
(with thanks to Christopher Logue)

I was about six, a rheumy kid, always ill. It was weak lungs, the doctor said, most likely caused by the foul blanket of smoke which brooded over the city from the belching chimneys. School kids laughed at me and called me a mummy's boy.

One dark and stormy evening, my mum and I were in the kitchen, where she was washing dishes under a cold tap (there was no hot one) and I was drying them. There was a loud knock at the front door. 'Who on earth could that be out on a night like this?' said my mum. She went to the door. A gaunt man, the wind tearing at his raincoat, stood there with a black leather box. He spoke to my mum and I heard her say, 'Blimey, I don't have a tanner [sixpence] to my name.' He said, 'For the boy, mum!' The rest of his words were swept away on the angry wind. 'Okay, come in,' she said. She found her purse and handed the man three pennies.

The man opened the shabby box and pulled out a white sheet which he tacked up on the kitchen wall. Then he took out a lantern with a spout at one end (the lense) and set it on the table. He placed a candle in the lantern and produced boxes filled with glass slides. He fed six of these into a metal bar and inserted it into the side of the lantern.

He asked my mother to turn off the light. I began to feel scared, when suddenly on the sheet ornate words appeared and the man began to read them in a melodious voice: 'The Adventures of Alice in Wonderland ... Alice sat on the bank when suddenly a white rabbit with pink eyes ran close by her ...' A new slide came up on the wall, a beautiful full-colour illustration of a white rabbit dressed in a check jacket, carrying an umbrella and looking at a pocket watch. '"Oh dear! I shall be late!" said the rabbit. Alice got up and ran after the rabbit and saw it pop down a large rabbit-hole under the hedge ...'

After twenty minutes the story ended. It was the most magically exhilarating time of my life, and Tenniel's magnificent illustrations haunted me. They became the yardstick by which to measure my own endeavours to become an illustrator – and still are.

Showing my work to London gallery owners in 1963. The drawings were on photographic paper, which made them hard to unravel.

GETTING ON THE LADDER

I'd been in Paris for three months. I'd read *On the Road* and it had seemed a good time to split the Big Smoke and become a beatnik in the city of lovers. Now, in the summer of 1963, I was on my way back to London, penniless. I was carrying a cardboard suitcase filled with drawings – portraits, mostly of people I'd drawn in bars or on the streets: dossers, vagrants, queer boys with bleeding-heart tattoos on their throats, hard-line junkies, beboppers, poppers, clochards, bohemian girls who were wannabe Juliette Grécos, jazz musicians, drag queens and assorted nutters. Drawings that I'd tried to sell to the sitters but couldn't even give away. It never occurred to me that the people I was sketching probably couldn't afford their next drink either.

I crossed on the Channel ferry from Calais to Dover. A violent storm came up out of nowhere and so did everyone's breakfast. I turned green and clung to a cafeteria table as the boat went up and down, up and down, over and over and over. When we docked at Dover I could hardly walk. I took the train to Victoria. It clattered through the drab, grey cityscape of south London and I wondered if I should have stayed in Paris.

I caught the Tube to Earl's Court, where I was to share a flat with an old mate, Keith. He forgot to tell me the place was above an Indian restaurant. It stank of curry and cardoman and within a few days so did we and all our clothes.

The only asset to my name, apart from an amazing old leather coat (which friends said looked like a dead horse) that I'd bought at a flea market in Paris, were my drawings. So I set out across London, cold-calling on art galleries. The problem with the drawings, apart from their amateur ineptness, was that they had been drawn on a roll of super heavyweight photographic paper, which had the perverse tendency to curl up and close like a venus fly trap when the drawings were removed from the suitcase. This made it virtually impossible to straighten out the drawings to show them to the effete chaps who ran the galleries.

Out of work, I was in Soho having a glass of bitter at the French House. A girl I knew, Wendy, came in lugging a huge flat bag. She told me that she was off to try her luck at getting a job at an art studio up the road. When it was time to leave, I offered to walk with her. The studio was in a back alley north of Goodge Street and looked dodgy. A dirty brass sign read 'Charlotte Studios'. Wendy decided to forget the interview. A light bulb went on in my head – why not let me borrow the bag and I'll go for the job?

I staggered up a dirty staircase with the large bag and into a dully lit, shambolic reception room. From the half light a charmless voice asked:

'What d'you want?'

'Wendy is ill, I work with her and have come for the job.'

My eyes got accustomed to the dimness and I saw a little man sitting at a desk eating a sandwich. He switched on an anglepoise lamp.

'Put your specimens here on the table.'

The word 'specimen' caught me by surprise; the only specimen I knew was the kind you gave to the doctor.

'I don't have all day,' rasped the little man, 'hurry yerself.'

I put the contents of the bag on the table: about ten boards with photos and type on them. He studied the top board.

'Did you draw this keyline?'

'Yes, sir,' I said, not knowing what a keyline was.

He moved to the next board and pointed to a photo.

'Did you "cow" this?'

'Yes, sir.' Cow? I hadn't a clue what that was either.

He continued through the boards with no more questions.

'Okay, what you looking for?'

'A job, sir.'

'Obviously! I meant salary. We have a position for a junior finished artist. Three pounds a week plus overtime. Hours 8.30 to 6 five days a week and 8.30 to 1 on Saturdays. No luncheon vouchers, and you supply your own steel rule and X-Acto knife.'

'I'll take it, sir.'

'When can you start?'

'Next Monday.'

'Don't be late.'

I couldn't believe my luck. I was on the art ladder, bottom rung, and the only way was up.

* * *

I showed up at 8.25 on the Monday, keen as mustard. I wore a white waiter's jacket and jeans. I thought I looked very cool.

A man (I learned later that he was the boss, Lucien) sat behind a desk in

Alan Aldridge, photographed by John Deakin, 1962.

Below *East End Street Musician*, 1963.
Opposite *Playground, Bethnal Green*, 1963.
**Some of my early paintings,
influenced by Ben Shahn's work.**

the shambolic room. The spilled light from the anglepoise made him to look like Satan. He stared at me.

'Are you the new boy?'

'Yes, sir.'

'Why are you dressed like that?'

Dressed like what? I'm sharp that's why.

Before I could reply, he barked:

'You look like a bloody ice-cream seller. Go home and come back wearing something decent.'

He waved me to get out. Decent, what's decent? I didn't have any other clothes. I borrowed a suit from Keith, it reeked of vindaloo and was three sizes too big for me. I got back to the studio by eleven o'clock.

Satan was still at the desk. He burst out laughing when I walked in.

'Christ, you look like a bloody refugee ... Oh my God, what's that smell?'

'It's the odour of curry, sir, absorbed into my suit. I live over an Indian restaurant.'

The little man who gave me the job came in. He screwed his face up.

'Ugh. Christ, has someone brought in an Indian takeaway?'

The Devil ripped into me.

'Be here tomorrow morning young man, respectably dressed and without the pungent odors of Hindu cooking. Or don't bother to come. GO.'

You step on the ladder and just as quickly you fall off.

I went to Alfie Kemp's on Camden High Street, a huge second-hand clothes store. They say nescessity is the mother of invention – I put on a well-fitting, three-piece, blue-pinstripe suit under the voluminous suit I was already wearing (could have put on two or three, it was so big) and walked out of the shop. Sorry, Alfie!

Next day I was in the studio at 8.25, dressed to the nines: blue suit and white shirt. The Devil saw me:

'This is an art studio, not a bloody bank.'

Oh no, I'm gonna be fired.

'But a great improvement. Go upstairs and find Tony, the studio manager, he'll put you to work. Did you bring a steel ruler and X-Acto knife?'

Whoops, I forgot.

'There's no art stores in Earl's Court. I'll go round the corner to Winsor and Newton in my lunch hour.'

'Don't forget. Go.'

I was back on the ladder and about to ascend faster than I could have ever imagined.

Upstairs the studio looked like something out of a Dickensian novel: the floor buckled and sagged dangerously, floorboards showed through the worn lino. Trash festered everywhere. There were five desks,

artists sat at four of them; they smelled of despair.

Tony greeted me and introduced the other artists. He sat me at the desk next to his and gave me a job bag.

'Your first job is to draw a sheep's digestive track. The client is Fison's, it's for their de-worming powder and will appear in an ad in *Farmers Weekly*.' He showed me a rough of what I had to draw and suggested I make the digestive tract keyline 0.7.

It was all double Dutch to me. I didn't understand a word and for the next hour shuffled papers, twiddled with my set square, sharpened pencils, stared blankly at my drawing pad and considered just walking out of the place and never coming back.

Finally Tony came over and whispered:

'You don't know what you're doing, do you?'

No point in beating about the bush. I confessed I didn't and to the duplicity I'd perpetrated to get the job. Much to my surprise, Tony volunteered to 'cover' for me. He would draw the sheep's innards and let me take the credit for it with the bosses.

Over the next nine months, thanks to Tony's ardent tutelage, I learned about keylines and cowing (the use of cow gum, a rubbery adhesive used to stick down photos), how to brush rule and retouch photos with an airbrush, to use Zippertone to fade and shade drawings, to colour-code printer's overlays and to draw lettering.

With a regular pay slip fattened with lots of overtime, I moved to a tiny loft in Heath Street (3A to be precise) in Hampstead and worked on drawings for my own book of specimens, which I'd need to move up the next few rungs of the ladder.

Untitled painting, 1963.

Cover illustrations
for *New Society*, 1964.
Top row, from left to
right 27 February,
3 December,
6 February.
Bottom row,
from left to right
20 August, 30 July.

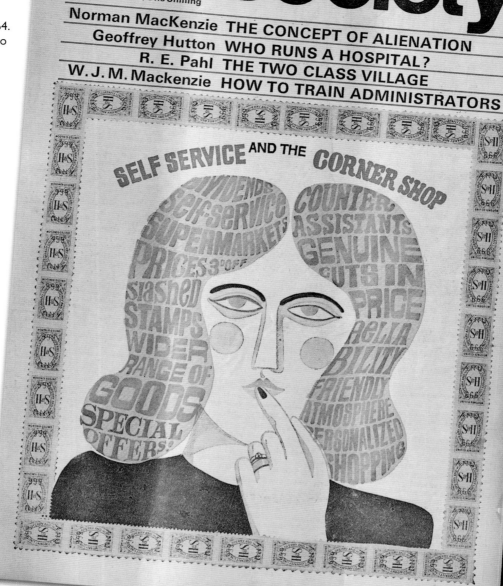

New society

27 Feb. 64/No.74/One Shilling

Norman MacKenzie THE CONCEPT OF ALIENATION
Geoffrey Hutton WHO RUNS A HOSPITAL?
R. E. Pahl THE TWO CLASS VILLAGE
W. J. M. Mackenzie HOW TO TRAIN ADMINISTRATORS

SELF SERVICE AND THE CORNER SHOP

HOT TO TROT

Charlotte Studios lasted nine months …
I got fired for dragging Lucien, the boss,
off a lavatory seat. Sounds ridiculous,
so let me explain.

Evening overtime was one big
funfair. The minute the bosses left,
around 6.30, the games began. There
were six of us, we'd split up into two
teams and cut heavyweight cardboard
into cigarette-card sized pieces. Each
man was allowed twenty cards. The
idea of the game was to place the card
between the index and middle finger,
then, using a lot of wrist action, flick it
at an opponent. In the right hands the
card became a sharp-edged missile
ready to tear out an eye, slice an ear –
three hits and you were out.

LAW REFORM /HARRY STREET

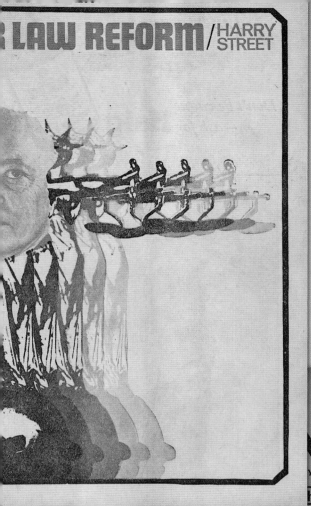

EAR AMERICA

HARRY STREET

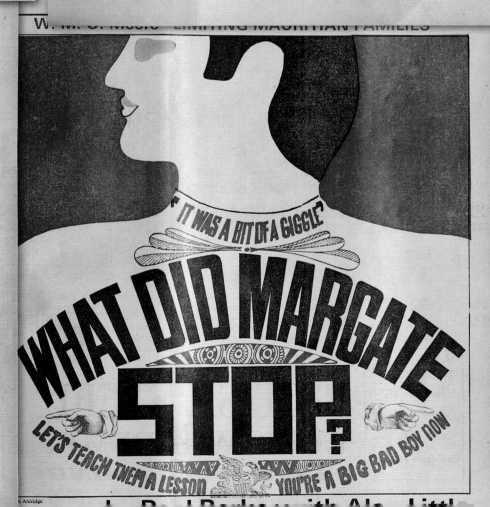

"IT WAS A BIT OF A GIGGLE"

WHAT DID MARGATE STOP?

LET'S TEACH THEM A LESSON — YOU'RE A BIG BAD BOY NOW

Illustrations for *New Society*, 1964.
Right Cover, 10 September.
Below 20 August.
Below right 6 February.

10 Sept 64/. No. 102/ 1s 3d weekly

Leonard Beaton	THE AVIATION TANGLE
Edmund Dell	CAN SCIENTISTS MANAGE ?
John A. Torode	LESLIE CANNON AND THE ETU
Kathleen Jones	TOO FEW PSYCHIATRIC BEDS
Donald Thomas	THE EROTICA WE DESERVE

DRUGS
SODA

38 WITNESSES

Alan Aldridge

AUGUST 1964

SEG
VOTE
L.B.J.
GOLDWATER

Alan Aldridge

SCHOOL
BOYCOTT
FREEDOM DAY FEBRUARY
JOIN THE ONE DAY BOYC

WE ARE THE HOLLOW MEN
WE ARE the STUFFED MEN
LEANING TOGETHER

VOTE CARD

VOTE

20 Hot to Trot

One team went to the front end of the studio and hunkered down behind desks, the other team went to the back and did the same. On the word 'go' fusilades of cards whistled back and forth across the studio. Frequent screams of 'Ouch you bastard!' attested to the deadly accuracy of both sides. Finally one team would win and we'd assemble to discuss the fast and furious action, some of the guys had bloody cuts sliced into their faces and lumpy bruises around the eyes.

Now came hide and seek. There were plenty of places to hide in the five ramshackle floors. I was 'it' so counted out loud to 100 then set off looking for those hiding. On a landing, I heard the noise of a stall door shutting in the lavatory. I crept up the stairs and slowly opened the door. The place was empty. On my left a urinal trough, to the right four stalls. All was silent. I knelt and looked under the partition of the stalls. In the end stall I saw a pair of spindly legs and trousers down around the ankles. One of the boys was sitting on the loo. This was too good to be true. Standing against the wall was a janitor's mop for cleaning the tiled floor. I grabbed it and snuck up to the stall. In one gorgeous movement, I shoved the mop under the stall, hooked it behind the feet of the occupant, and gave it an almighty yank. The feet flew upwards and a

Above First illustration for the *Sunday Times* magazine, 'Psychology & Psychiatry Reviews', 17 January 1964.
Below The original artwork.

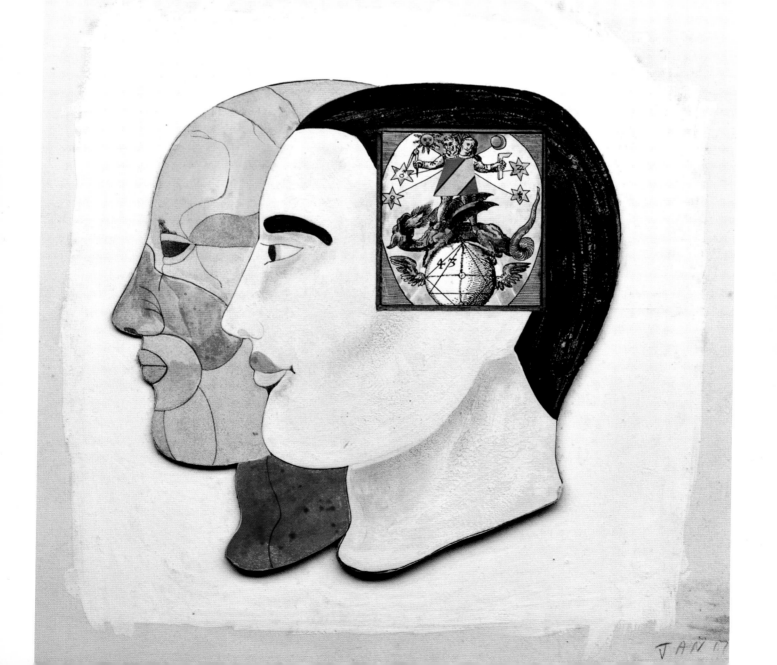

Above *Sunday Times* magazine, 1965.
I was commissioned to do an illustration for an article about a romantic dinner made from refrigerated food. So I went down to a junk yard I knew in the East End and bought a pre-war refrigerator (I loved the bell-shaped part on top) and hauled it by truck to my studio. I spent the weekend decorating it with a pair of lovers and the food mentioned in the article. On Monday morning the fridge was delivered to the *Sunday Times*'s studio to be photographed – word went out that I was mad, and I heard that the word 'genius' got whispered too …

Opposite Illustration for *MacBird* by Barbara Garson, 1966.
This was an anti-establishment play, which parodied *Macbeth* and attacked President Lyndon B. Johnson (the MacBird in the title). I showed him haunted by his predecessor, John F. Kennedy.

certain amount of bare flesh and private parts skidded into view.

Someone yelled, 'What the hell is going on?'

Whoops, it wasn't one of the boys … it was the Devil himself, Lucien the boss. What the hell was he doing here?

I bolted downstairs. Amazingly all the other artists were diligently working at their desks. I guess they'd seen Lucien come into the building. I sat at my desk and had barely picked up my Rapidograph when Lucien stormed in, red as a beetroot, spitting fire and brimstone.

'Who attacked me in the lavatory? Which of you idiots yanked me off the toilet?'

There was an audible swell of giggles among us as Lucien raged on:

'You're all fired if someone doesn't own up.'

Barely able to talk for laughing, I fessed up and got fired instantly.

I got a job in a coffee bar, the Nucleus in Covent Garden. It meant late nights – it was a shooting gallery for heroin addicts. After work I'd go to Bunjies, a much gentler place on Litchfield Street. They had a wall covered in flyers, one, headed 'Graphic Workshop', advertised an eight-week evening coarse taught by Bob Gill, Romek Marber, Tony Palladino, Lou Klein, Robert Brownjohn, Germano Facetti, Marcello Minale and Brian Tattersfield, among others. They were big names in the graphics business, although totally unknown to me. The price was a tenner and here was the clincher – students who couldn't afford the fee could sit at the back for free, with coffee on the house.

I went for the free coffee.

The students were all advertising types: grey suits, ties and button-down shirts. The lectures went from the boring, 'The need for uniformity and clarity in road signage' to the ultra boring, 'How to integrate serif and sans-serif typefaces in educational publications'. Romek Marber waffled on in a thick Polish accent (which few could understand) about the mathematical structure of his design grid for the Penguin crime series. 'From Bodoni to Bookman' had F. H. K. (Henri) Henrion in raptures on the history of typefaces; Brownjohn talked in his alcohol-fuelled voice on the advertising masterpieces of Doyle Dane Bernbach; Bob Gill ripped British design to shreds

(I did like his work though); Brian Tattersfield eulogized about Swiss design, though I think it's probably the most overlauded, boring style ever foisted on the British.

At the end of the evening an assignment was set and then reviewed the following week. The last exercise was to design a cover for *The Best Detective Stories of Cyril Hare*, in the Penguin crime series. The winning design would be used for real and along with that kudos would be a £25 prize – three weeks' wages plus overtime.

Just my luck, I was getting married the coming weekend, then going off to Aldeburgh for a week's honeymoon – I was out of the running, or was I? I got married, went on honeymoon, then on the Tuesday evening told Rita, my new wife, that we were out of money (which we were just about) and couldn't afford to stay at the hotel any longer. Wednesday we were back in our new flat in Belsize Park and I hurriedly put together a rough for the Penguin book cover – a collage of clocks, tits, eyeballs, keys, shadows – and took it to the final class of the Graphic Workshop on the Thursday evening … and it won!

Germano Facetti (art director at Penguin Books) took me under his wing. I became his 'graphical gofer', not only putting together his cover ideas for Penguin but also working on his freelance work. I loved biking down the hill from my little flat to Germano's huge Victorian house in Camden Town. His whole ground floor was one large studio, the walls either lined floor to ceiling with art books or festooned with Eduardo Paolozzi prints and Bill Brandt photos – the studio even had the luxury of an espresso machine.

Work from Germano came thick and fast, mostly Penguin covers that he needed urgently to present to the cover committee the following day. He also handed me the responsibility of designing the window display for Better Books every couple of weeks, a hip store started by Tony Godwin, who was chief editor at Penguin Books. Facetti volunteered to design brochures for free for the newly formed Design and Art Directors' Association, then handed the assignments over to me.

There was a wonderful social side to hanging out with Germano; I got to meet Francis Bacon, Frank Auerbach, Enzo Apicella, Lucian Freud, the booze-bemused John Deakin and innumerable denizens of Soho at Wheeler's on Old Compton Street, where we had champagne and oysters. Then we'd go to the dingy dive called the Colony Room, secreted away up a gloomy stairwell, stinking of rotting food from the kitchens of Quo Vadis.

(An aside. Some years later, at the Arthur Tooth Gallery, I had a few pieces of work in a group show with other artists, including Francis Bacon. At the opening, standing with me and a few others in front of my work, Francis said, 'Alan is the only artist I know who never learned how to draw a straight line.' It got a laugh. Still does.)

The urbane Germano drank Pernod at the French House and held court at La Terrazza – its clean, white interior designed by Enzo Apicella with nary a dangling Chianti bottle in sight. It was the first restaurant in London to serve authentic southern Italian cuisine. I ate Italian food for the first time (unless you count tins of Heinz spaghetti). Vitello tonnato and spaghetti bolognese were washed down with glasses of Pinot Grigio, finishing with zabaglioni. Already Charlotte Studios was becoming a distant memory. My bank manager got friendlier by the minute as I paid in cheques on a daily basis to my ever expanding account. I'd gone from half-hour lunches at Bernardo's coffee bar – gobbling down a sweaty Kraft cheese slice between stale bread with a cuppa tea – to poncing around fancy restaurants *mange*-ing delicious food with names I couldn't pronounce.

And it got better.

In 1964 Germano received a commission from Lord Snowdon to design his new book of photographs, to be called *Private View*. It showed artists, their art and studios, and John Russell, the distinguished art critic of the *Sunday Times*, was set to write the words. I would put together the layouts for the publisher, based on Germano's scribbles. Since Snowdon was then married to Princess Margaret, this meant trips to Kensington Palace.

On my first visit, I had to be accompanied by John Russell. I met him at his home in St John's Wood, where he gave me a quick lesson in the etiquette of meeting royalty, and then off we went in a cab. At the gates to Kensington Palace we were 'okayed' by the police and as we arrived at the front door it opened and there stood Princess Margaret ready to greet us.

Jeez, I was expecting a uniformed flunky. Flummoxed, I forgot the etiquette lessons. I turned to John for pointers but he was down on one knee, head bowed, forehead almost touching the ground in supplication, looking quite ridiculous. I didn't remember that lesson either. I introduced myself and lightly shook hands with the Princess. She ordered John to his feet, then led us through the palace to Lord Snowdon's office, a large, airy room filled with antiques, fine Old Masters and a long desk strewn with photos.

Lord Snowdon greeted us, insisting that we call him Tony (Antony Armstrong-Jones was the name by which he'd become known as a photographer). There were handshakes all round and then we got down to business. Tony explained my role: I would come to the palace a couple of times a week to prepare finished layouts using photographs printed to size which would be sent to the publisher – my expertise at 'cowing', learned in the trenches of Charlotte Studios was going to be put to good use.

I became a regular visitor to Kensington Palace over a two-month period. I have two particular memories of those visits. I was in Snowdon's studio (he was out of town on a photo assignment) and had to crop some photos and 'cow' them to the publisher's production sheets. The studio table was overcrowded with photos and negatives, so I looked round for somewhere to work and found a small lacquered table. Using a scalpel and a steel rule I began hacking up photos. Five minutes into this Princess Margaret walked in. She asked if I'd like a cup of tea. Then she noted what I was doing and with the coolness of a cucumber said:

'Alan, would you mind not cutting on that, it's a fifteenth-century Ming dynasty table.'

She left to get my cup of tea. I lifted the photos and saw that the top of the table – an ornate, gold-lacquered painting – was hacked to shreds.

On another occasion, I had worked from mid-afternoon to early evening preparing page spreads for the publisher, eaten supper (pheasant and chips) in the palace kitchen, and was tidying up ready to go home when Princess Margaret, wearing a beautiful yellow silk cocktail dress, invited me to

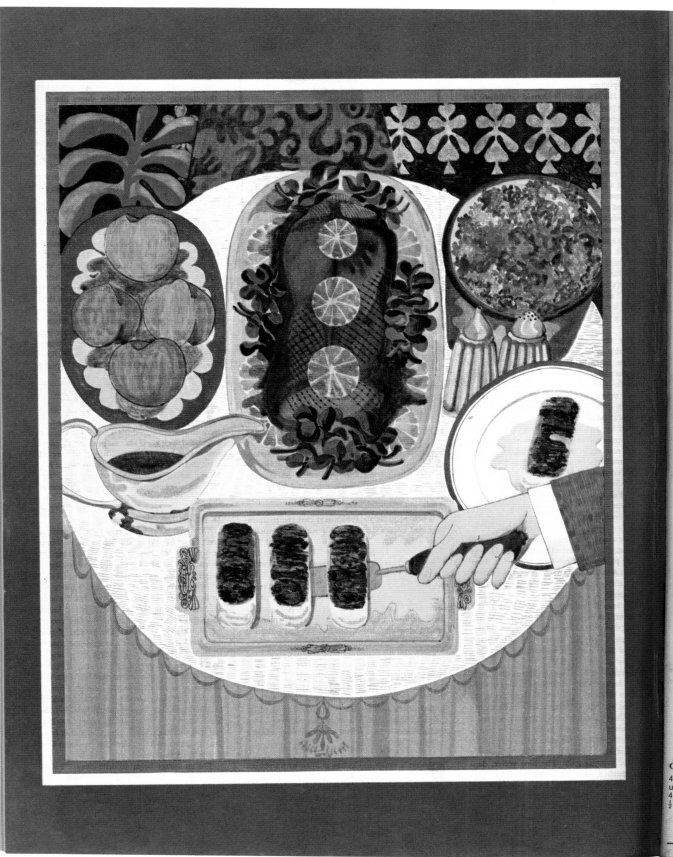

This meal is wha[...]
themselves are orn[...]
observes the classic[...]
what to eat with [...]
It begins with the [...]
They have such a [...]
some kind, which s[...]
a smooth cheese sa[...]
a sauce and this im[...]
grand. We have f[...]
Edwardians who a[...]
sauce wi[...] a brow[n...]

TURBOT QUEN[...]
PÂTE À CHOUX M[...]
3 fluid oz. milk/3 flu[...]
1 tablespoon butter,[...]
3 oz. sifted flour/2 e[...]

QUENELLE MIXTUR[...]
1¼ lb. turbot (after s[...]
been removed)/2 oz.[...]
2 egg yolks/8 tables[...]
2 egg whites/salt, w[...]
nutmeg/Cognac

TO POACH QUENE[...]
Butter/flour/salted w[...]

CANARD BRAISÉ
1 tender duckling (5-6[...]
salt and freshly-groun[...]
6 tablespoons butter/[...]
1 tablespoon sugar/1[...]
juice of 1 orange/¼ pi[...]
4 oranges, peeled and[...]
watercress, to garnish[...]

COMPOTE OF PEAC[...]
4 ripe peaches/4 thin s[...]
unpeeled/¾ pint water/[...]
4 tablespoons sugar
½ teaspoon vanilla esse[...]

Illustrations for the *Sunday Times* magazine.
Opposite *Ageing!*, 1967.

Above 'Robert Carrier plans a meal (1),
27 June 1965.

Book covers for the publisher
Anthony Blond.
Powdered Eggs by Charles Simmons, 1965.
The Leader by Gillian Freeman, 1965.
Opposite Unpublished artwork, *c.* 1965.

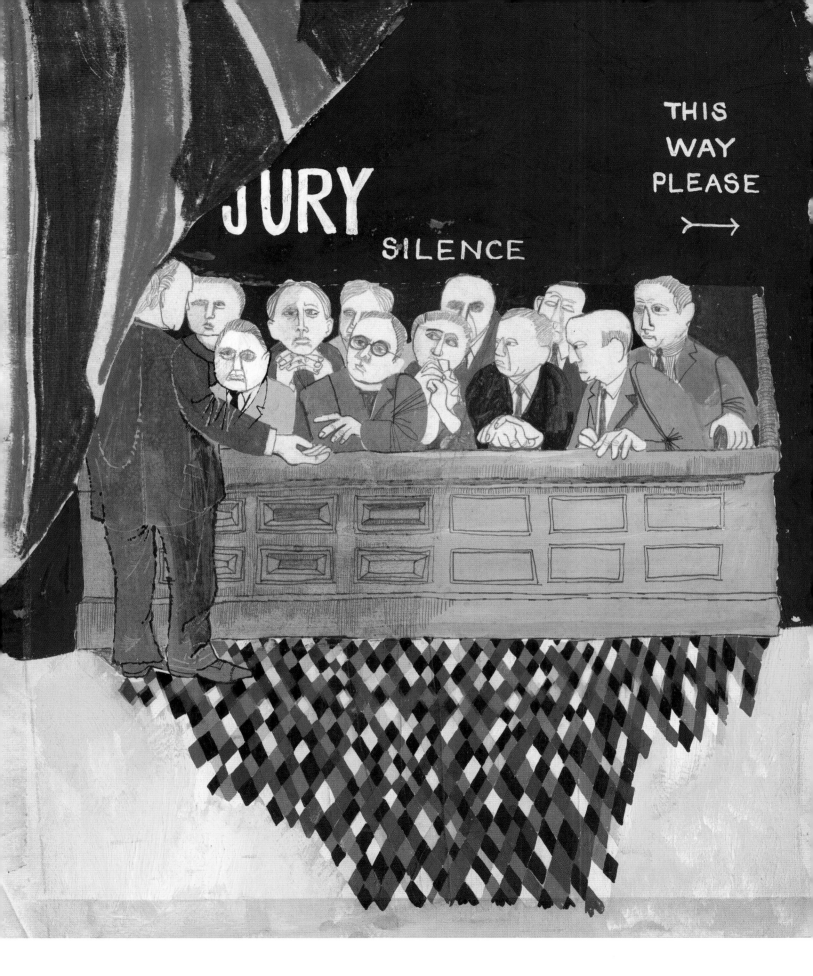

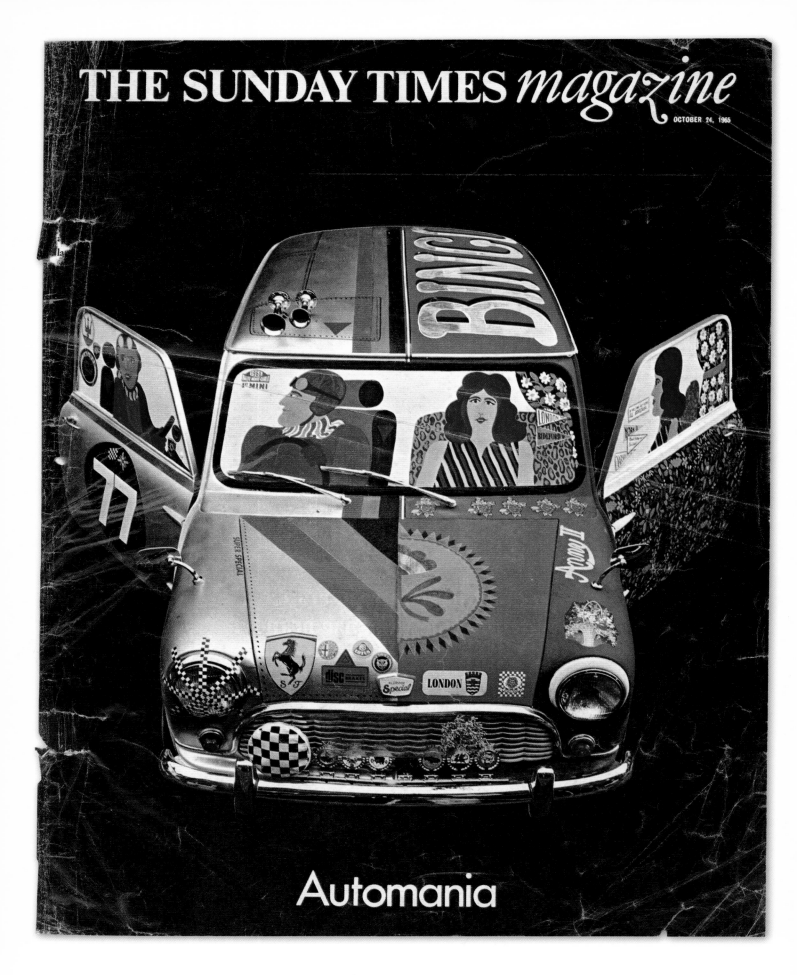

THE SUNDAY TIMES *magazine*

OCTOBER 24, 1965

Automania

join her for a cocktail. I followed her into what I'd call a drawing room. A servant entered with two drinks – Martinis.

We clinked glasses and I sipped my drink. It was horrible, the first cocktail I'd ever had. I'd have to grin and bear it. Princess Margaret's went down in one swig. We chitchatted for a few minutes, and all the while I was thinking, if my mum could see me now, she'd be running up and down her street yelling, 'My Alan, he's at the palace having drinks with Princess Margaret ... he's at the pal ...'

'Would you like to listen to some music? I have my father's record collection here.'

The question interrupted my mummy reverie. Her father's record collection – that must be King George VI's. Who could say no to that? She went to a large old-fashioned radiogram and stacked some 78s on the record changer. I was thinking it'll be Beethoven or Elgar but was surprised when Frankie Laine came on singing the theme from 'Rawhide'. More drinks arrived; I was still sipping my first. The records, all American singers, kept playing and I continued to chinwag with Margaret for half an hour or so.

'Do you dance, Alan?' said the Princess.

Well, I did – I had a bronze medal for ballroom dancing. See, I'd got into a little bit of trouble as a teenager and the judge, bless him, had decided that a trip to Borstal wasn't on the cards so he sentenced me to a stint at the Ron and Doris Kerr School of Ballroom Dancing for as long as it took me to get a bronze medal. So I had to attend classes three nights a week and get Ron or Doris to sign me in and out, then take that chit and register it at the local police station – to keep me off the streets.

'Yes, ma'am, bit of a snake hips, if I say so meself.' That was the Martini talking – I was on my second. She laughed and changed records: Nat King Cole, 'When I Fall In Love', gentle, dreamy music. She held up her arms and smiled ... I lightly took her right hand and put my other hand around her waist. Then I was trying to figure out if the music was a waltz or a quickstep while thinking that if my mum could see me now she'd be running up and down the City Road, in and out of the Eagle, 'My Alan's dancing with Princess Margaret ... dancing with ... '

Illustrations for the *Sunday Times* magazine.
Opposite Cover, 24 October 1965.
Above 'Robert Carrier plans a meal 2', 4 July 1965.
Left 'Robert Carrier plans a meal 3' (Aldridge/Croxford), 11 July 1965.
Below left 'Robert Carrier plans a meal 4', 18 July 1965.
Below right 'Mushroom and bacon' (for Robert Carrier), 7 March 1965.

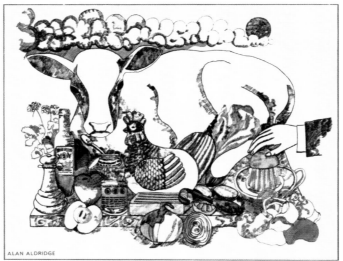

Waltz or quickstep, it didn't matter, we simply danced on the spot, a sort of smooch-like slow dance. When the song ended we separated.

'Thank you, Alan, snake hips indeed! Now I must get ready for the theatre.'

A few minutes later I was in a cab heading north to Parliament Hill. What a night.

Oh yeah, one last thing. Lord Snowdon recommended me to the creative director of the *Sunday Times* art department, just about the hottest studio in London. I got a job there as a junior 'visualizer' – it was a job of a lifetime. Little did I know that in less than a year I'd become the fiction cover art director at Penguin Books.

Old Hall, New Hall
Michael Innes

A Guide to English Schools
Tyrrell Burgess

After I'd won first prize at the Graphic Workshop I started doing three or four covers a week for Germano Facetti (art director at Penguin) – soon he was touting me around town as the most original designer in London! In 1965, his boss, Tony Godwin (the brilliant chief editor), phoned to ask if I knew any American art directors (Americans were flavour of the month, pouring into London – Bob Gill, Robert Brownjohn, Tony Palladino, Lou Klein – and pinching all the best jobs!) who could take over the fiction covers from Germano. I told him I didn't know any Americans but there was one bloke who could do the job.

'Who?' he asked.

'Me!'

We both laughed. Two weeks later Tony called to offer me the job. I told him I could take it only if Germano agreed. So it came to pass that I started at Penguin. I was given a big studio in John Street and hand-picked my staff. Tony wanted Penguin fiction to compete more aggressively in the market place and that attitude drove us for two years – but just over the horizon I could hear the Penguin board sharpening their knives ...

Covers for Penguin Books, 1964–65. **These were done before I became fiction cover art director there. Crime titles were green, Pelicans (non-fiction titles) blue and fiction** orange, or sometimes red (see overleaf). These early illustrations all used Romek Marber's cover template.

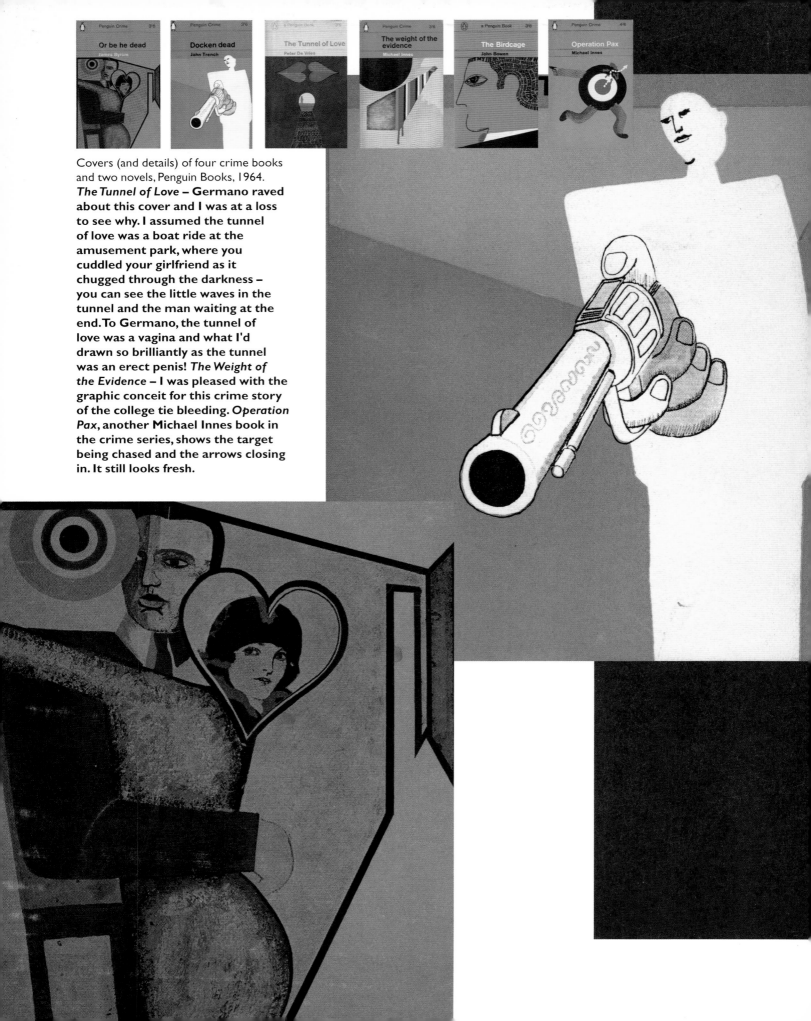

Covers (and details) of four crime books and two novels, Penguin Books, 1964.
The Tunnel of Love – **Germano raved about this cover and I was at a loss to see why. I assumed the tunnel of love was a boat ride at the amusement park, where you cuddled your girlfriend as it chugged through the darkness – you can see the little waves in the tunnel and the man waiting at the end. To Germano, the tunnel of love was a vagina and what I'd drawn so brilliantly as the tunnel was an erect penis!** *The Weight of the Evidence* – **I was pleased with the graphic conceit for this crime story of the college tie bleeding.** *Operation Pax*, **another Michael Innes book in the crime series, shows the target being chased and the arrows closing in. It still looks fresh.**

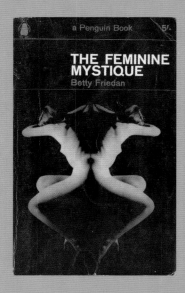

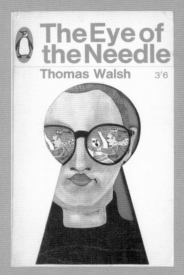

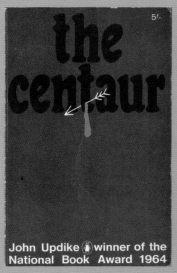

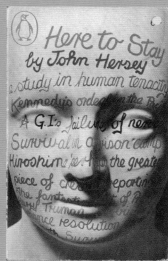

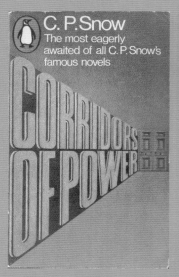

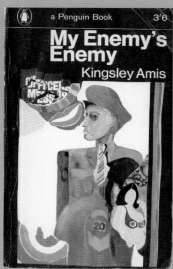

A selection of Penguin covers, 1965–67.
The Feminine Mystique – I shot a nude and flip-flopped it to suggest a Rorschach test, in keeping with the psychological tone of the book. *Invisible Man*, a truly great book. For the cover, I painted two white business men shaking hands on a deal, not noticing that there was a black man standing between them. *The Eye of the Needle*, a priest witnesses a murder. *Kiss Kiss*, a typical Dahl collection of macabre stories. This is one of my favourite covers and shows a man being minced; the mince was real – a pound of ground fillet steak. After the shoot I went on holiday for a week. When I got back I opened the door to the studio and a million bloated black flies poured out, followed by the stench of rotten meat. I'd forgotten to throw away the mince. *Am I Too Loud? The Memoirs of a Piano Accompanist*. For this I shot a group of composers' busts (available in any classical music store) with headphones. *The Garrick Year* – Rita, my first wife, was a big Margaret Drabble fan and had a nice surprise when I put a photo I'd taken of her on the front cover. *Girls in their Married Bliss*. The author's name was more prominent than the title. In the mid-sixties Edna O'Brien was a literary star. I met her to show her the cover; I think she liked it. I certainly fancied her.

Penguin sci-fi titles needed a face-lift. I started by creating a distinctive alphabet with a futuristic feel – Harry Willock was the lettering artist. The first title was *The Wind from Nowhere*. I chose a black background to enhance the colour. Having the buildings bend towards the spine may have influenced me to reverse the artwork.

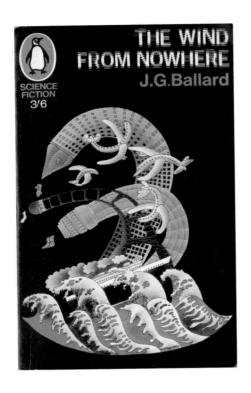

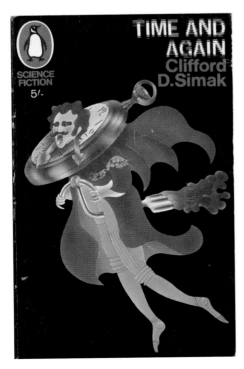

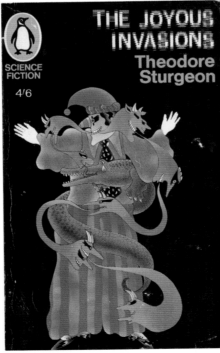

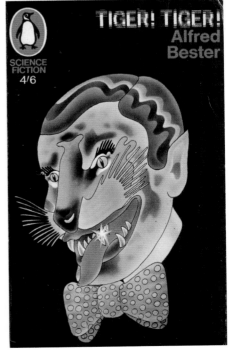

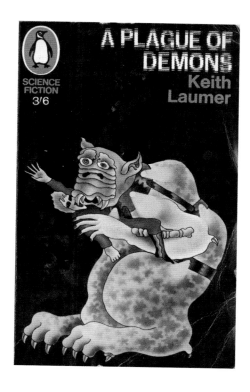

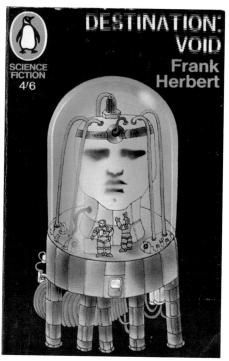

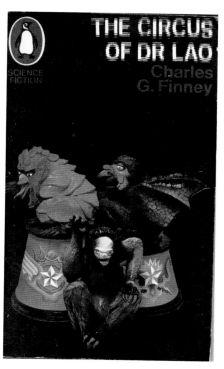

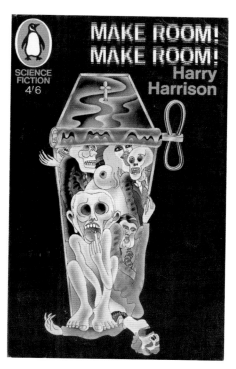

Cover (and detail) of the first edition of
The Penguin Book of Comics, written with
George Perry, 1967.

Chapter numbers and illustrations from *The Penguin Book of Comics*, 1967.

The *Penguin Book of Comics* evolved out of my love of English comics. I pitched the idea of a history of comics to Tony Godwin and he okayed it right away, including the size, roughly 11 x 8", a first for Penguin. I asked George Perry, assistant editor of the *Sunday Times* magazine, to write it and I couldn't have asked for anyone better. When the first copies arrived, Tony and I took one to Sir Allen Lane, the Penguin founder. We were ushered into his office and I held up the book for him to see – his face went from charming to alarming, 'That is not a Penguin,' he snarled and Tony and I retreated. I felt that Penguin did not promote the book but a second edition came out four years later.

NOVA

FEBRUARY 1966 THREE SHILLINGS

WE REGRET TO ANNOUNCE THAT IT IS POSSIBLE THAT 1.8 OF OUR READERS WILL BE MURDERED THIS YEAR

THESE, OF COURSE, ARE ONLY THE ONES WHO WILL BE DISCOVERED. SEE PAGE 20

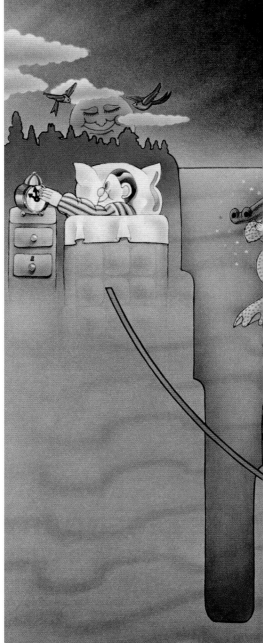

Nova, February 1966.
Above Cover.
Right Inside page showing the strangler.
**This cover was intended to shock.
Nova, radical and anti-establishment, carved a deep swathe through the lacklustre world of women's magazines of the day. Dennis Hackett, a blunt northener, was the editor and the magazine's driving force. He wrote the headline on the cover and asked me to illustrate it. I painted the** grinning man, photographed it, then **projected the 35mm shot onto a girl's frightened face. Droves of readers refused to buy the issue because the cover was both offensive and disturbing – not as much as it was for those who bought it and turned to the page with the smiling strangler staring at them with real glass eyes through granny glasses, leering yellow dentures, and hands as the bodies of his victims.**

Above *Night Voyage*, 'Each night's sleep is broken into four or five intervals of dreaming ... The curve shows the body temperature.' *Sunday Times* magazine, 16 February 1969.

Left Sammy Speedyfeet, 1966.
I read that children using the traditional roller skate, with its high centre of gravity, often twisted or broke their ankles. I patented a shoe skate where the axle was placed through the re-inforced sole and heel of the shoe, rather than below. I called the skate Sammy Speedyfeet.

Design and Art Direction '66

Above *Design and Art Direction '66*, the annual of the fourth exhibition of the Design & Art Directors' Association, London, published by Studio Vista, London.

Cover design by Alan Aldridge and Lou Klein.

Opposite Alan Aldridge and his son Miles, photographed by Snowdon in 1968.

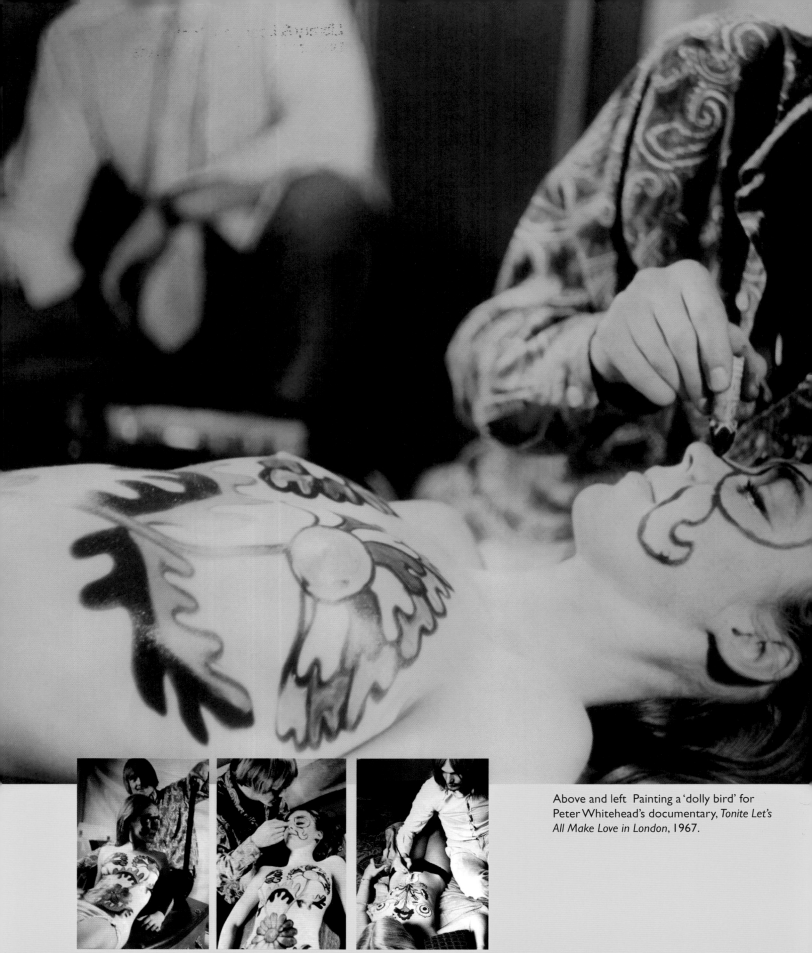

Above and left Painting a 'dolly bird' for
Peter Whitehead's documentary, *Tonite Let's
All Make Love in London*, 1967.

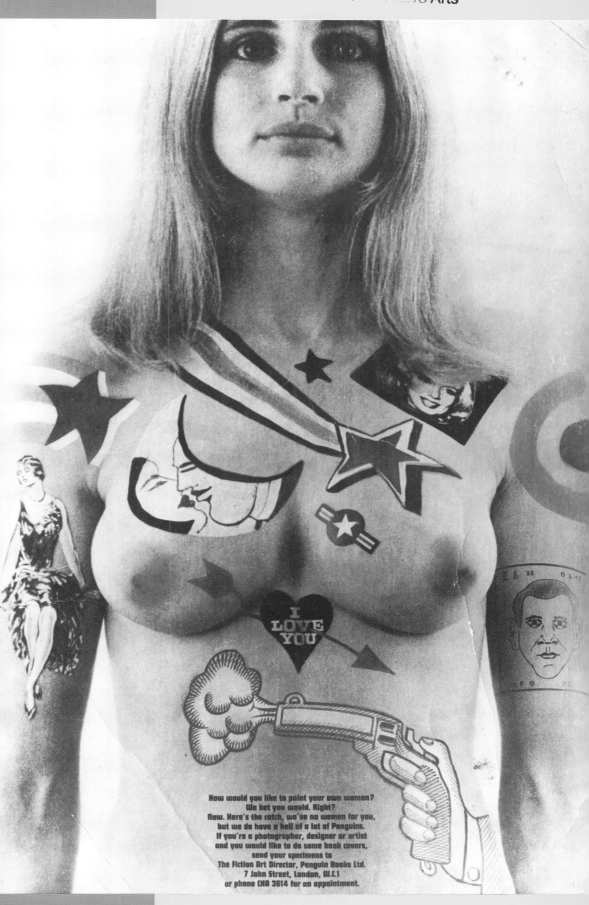

How would you like to paint your own woman?
We bet you would. Right?
Now. Here's the catch, we've no women for you,
but we do have a hell of a lot of Penguins.
If you're a photographer, designer or artist
and you would like to do some book covers,
send your specimens to
The Fiction Art Director, Penguin Books Ltd.
7 John Street, London, W.C.1
or phone CHA 3614 for an appointment.

Right **In 1967 I was asked to paint a naked lady for Penguin Books, to be used in a job advertisement for cover designers. It didn't go down too well with the company's founder, Sir Allen Lane, but it got an enthusiastic response from art students all over Britain.**

The Beatles, dream-weavers of the mythic sixties, became a major influence on my life and early career. It all began in 1966. I met John Lennon first. I'd done illustrations for *Nova* magazine based on the song titles of the Beatles LP *Revolver*. John rang me out of the blue and said he really liked my work. He came over to my studio and saw more of it. A few weeks later he asked me to do the cover for *The Penguin John Lennon*, a compilation of his two hugely successful books, *In His Own Write* and *A Spaniard in the Works*. My original idea was to do Lennon dressed up as a penguin but that was not deemed suitable by the management at Penguin Books. Then I thought of a photograph of Lennon as Superman. He was, after all, bigger than Jesus Christ. We arranged to meet at Duffy's, an excellent but expensive photographer who was delighted 'to shoot yer actual Beatle' though less impressed by the £50 fee. For the session I made models in Plasticine of characters from the books, painted mad eyes on granny spectacles and tailored up a Superman outfit – for a couple of hours John posed with enthusiasm, then announced, 'Gotta go!', combed his hair and rushed off in his Rolls. DC Comics would not let us reproduce the Superman logo so in the finished version the letters on the front of John's outfit were changed to 'J L'.

Opposite Back and front covers of
The Penguin John Lennon, 1967.

Right Drawing of John Lennon as a penguin, which was the original concept.

Above and below Outtakes from Brian Duffy's photo shoot.

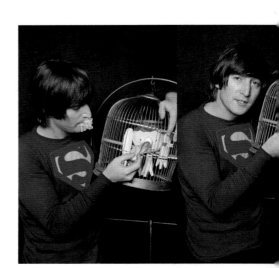

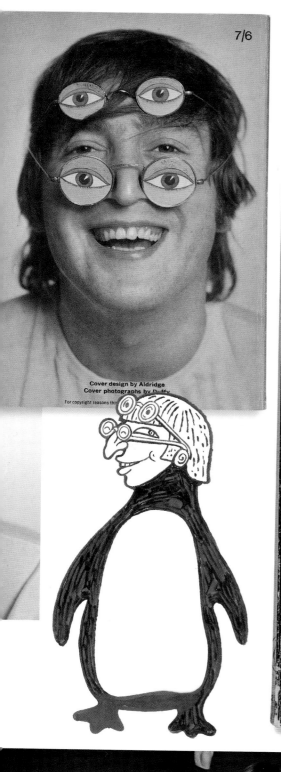

7/6

Cover design by Aldridge
Cover photographs by Duffy

For copyright reasons this

THE PENGUIN

John Lennon

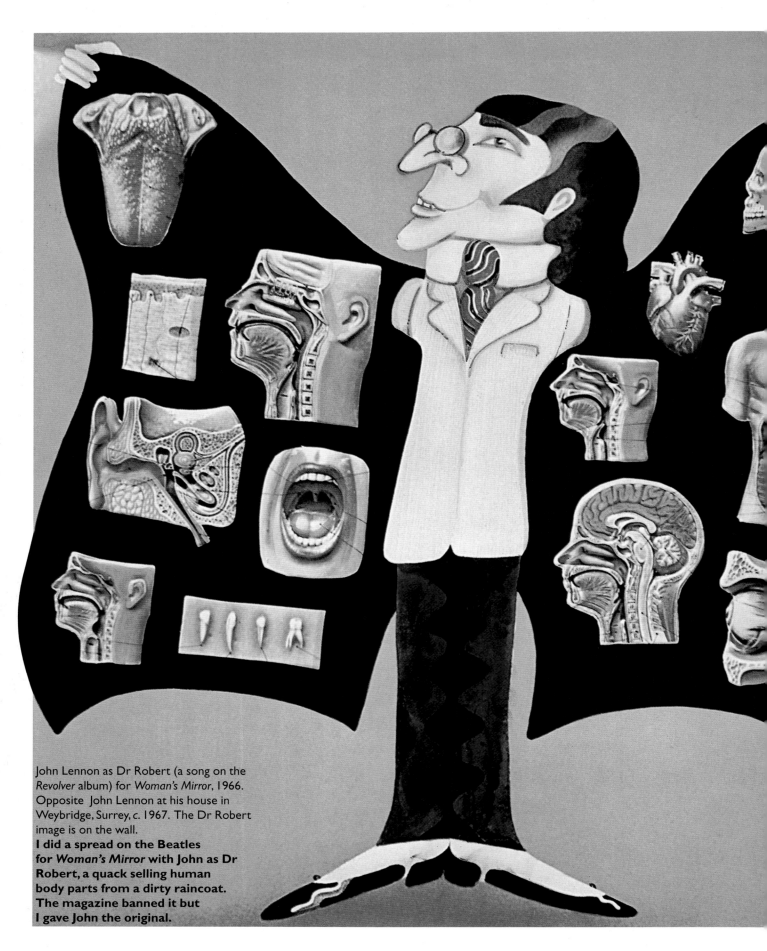

John Lennon as Dr Robert (a song on the *Revolver* album) for *Woman's Mirror*, 1966. Opposite John Lennon at his house in Weybridge, Surrey, *c.* 1967. The Dr Robert image is on the wall.

I did a spread on the Beatles for *Woman's Mirror* with John as Dr Robert, a quack selling human body parts from a dirty raincoat. The magazine banned it but I gave John the original.

It was the Summer of Love – 1967. The sounds of *Sgt Pepper*, the sweet reek of 'grass' and joss sticks was everywhere. Groovy chicks in thin summery dresses and no bras invited 'free love'. It was good to be alive.

PAUL McCARTNEY

I was at my studio and Barry Fantoni (a cartoonist for Private Eye) was rabbiting on about how the title of the Beatles' song 'Lucy in the Sky with Diamonds' really meant LSD (Lysergic Acid Diethylamide). John Lennon vehemently denied this, saying the song was based on a drawing by his son Julian of Lucy O'Donnell, a friend at nursery school. Yeah, right, John, and I was born under a gooseberry bush.

Mmm ... my mind clicked into 'make a quick-buck mode'. I wondered if there were any other references to sex, drugs and perversions hidden among the *Sgt Pepper* lyrics and if so what a great magazine article it would make. I mentioned this to Barry who responded matter of factly that he had Paul's home phone number and why didn't I call and ask him. He read me the number. I dialled it, expecting it to ring forever (no answering machines back then) or for a butler to answer saying Mr McCartney was recording at Abbey Road Studios and would I leave a message. It hadn't reached the second ring before a familiar voice with a Liverpudlian accent answered:

' 'allo?'

Jeeeeesus Christ, it's Lord God Almighty, the guv'nor, Beatle Paul. He was the last person I'd expected to pick up the phone.

'Ah, um, 'allo Paul, Alan Aldridge here.'

'Hey. How are yer?' Said as if he'd known me for years.

'Yeah, fine. Was wondering if I could sort of do an interview with you – go through the *Sgt Pepper* lyrics, you know, discuss how they got written – what were their influences, etc?'

'Sure.'

'Yeah.'

'Why don't you come over now?'

Whoa! This was happening way too fast.

'What, like now?'

'Sure.'

Who said 'He who hesitates is lost'?

'Okay I'll be there in half an hour.'

I put the phone down and immediately realized that I hadn't asked Paul for his address. And as he was the most famous bloke (well, equal with John) in the world, I was sure it was a much-guarded secret. I'd just have to call him back. I did and he wasn't picking up. Damn, I'd messed up big time. When I told Barry my predicament, he knew Paul's address as if it was his grandmother's – he'd been to the house on several occasions.

I called Radio Cabs – a taxi arrived in less than five minutes. I jumped in and asked for Cavendish Avenue, St John's Wood. The driver checked out my long hair, tight jeans and snakeskin jacket.

'You goin' to Paul's?'

'Um. Yeah.'

So much for the address being secret.

In the comfort of the black cab I suddenly felt a vague sense of panic. I'd never done an interview and didn't do shorthand. Plus, I knew only a couple of songs from *Sgt Pepper*: 'A Day in the Life' and 'Being for the Benefit of Mr Kite'. I needed to stop and buy the album. All was not lost – I had a brilliant idea.

'Cabbie, I need to stop at Imhoffs.'

Now Imhoffs wasn't exactly on the way but I could kill two birds with one stone – buy the album and purchase a tape recorder for the interview. Imhoffs was on the corner of New Oxford Street and Tottenham Court Road and not only stocked records but had the best electronics department in London. I ran in, got the album, no problem, and went up the escalator to the electronics department. The place was busy. I collared a salesman and breathlessly told him I was in a great hurry and needed a portable tape recorder, the best he'd got for an interview. He unequivocally recomended a Uher 4000 reel-to-reel and laid a beautiful cube of brushed aluminium, festooned with dials and nobs, on the counter in front of me.

'Twenty-one pounds – it's the very best we have.'

It looked seriously professional, just the ticket.

'I'll take it.'

I peeled off two tenners and and a oncer and was ready to split.

'Let me give sir a demonstration.'

''S'okay, I'm in a hurry.'

'It'll take just a couple of minutes.'
He began fiddling with various nobs.
'Has sir used a Uher before?'
'No, never. Never done an interview either.'
'Oh. May I ask who sir is interviewing? Someone in the pop culture world?'
'Nobody important, just some slushy "moon in June" songwriter. I've really gotta go.'
The salesman squealed:
'Sir, no way, you need to understand …'
He grabbed the Uher and was about to recommence the demonstration. I yanked it from his hands, stuffed the machine in my shoulder bag and legged it down the stairs to the waiting cab. Jeez, how hard is it to switch a tape recorder on and off?
Paul's residence was no secret. When we got to Cavendish Avenue about a hundred pubescent girls milled about

outside the tall gates of his house, grasping pictures of Paul, autograph books and banners: 'Love You Paul', 'Paul Marry Me', 'Paul Rules'. I got out of the cab and a girl yelled, 'It's Brian Jones' and instantly I was at the centre of a cyclone of sexually fevered girls, clawing and molesting me. A nice London constable came to my rescue – warning the girls that their behaviour would get them arrested. The fans backed off.
The bobby accompanied me to the gate and I pressed the bell. A voice said:
'Yeah?'
'Hello, Alan Aldridge.'
'C'mon in.'
The gates opened and I hurried up the steps to the house. Paul opened the front door and we small-talked along a corridor of framed Magrittes to a spacious room at the back of the house. We sat on a large settee facing

each other. We had a cup of tea, chinwagged and shared a joint for about fifteen minutes …
'I've got three hours then gorra go to an art show with Jane [Asher], so wanna get started?'
'Sure.'
I got the Uher out of my shoulder bag and placed it between us.
'D'you mind if I record the interview?'
'No problem.'
Now for the first time I studied the tape deck expecting to see nobs marked 'Play', 'Stop', 'Rewind', 'Fast Forward', 'Volume', 'Tone'. Instead they were marked with incomprehensible symbols: a black dot, a half moon, two squiggles like a pair of worms mating, a circle with spikes that resembled an alchemical alembic. I was in trouble. For a couple of the longest minutes I've ever sat through I fiddled with nobs, checked reels and generally pretended I knew what I was doing. Finally, Paul queried:

'Have you used this machine before?'

'Sure, many times, interviewed Allen Ginsberg with it last week.'

Both statements not true. I was digging a hole for myself and it was getting bigger by the minute.

'The reels seem to be stuck.'

I ventured to buy a bit more time and continued turning dials up and down in a hopeless attempt to get the machine working. Paul showed no impatience and let me fiddle while Rome burned for another minute or so then suggested that he take a look. Master of all things musical, he touched a control knob and immediately an arrow in one of the dials jumped into action. Touched another and we heard the whirr of tape rewinding.

'Just check you've got nothing on the tape.'

Paul pressed a button. Ambient noise crackled from the speakers, then came the voice of the salesman from Imhoffs: 'demonstration', then me: "S'okay, I'm in a hurry.' Salesman again: 'It'll take just a couple of minutes ... Has sir used a Uher before?' Now idiot me: 'No, never. Never done an interview either.' 'May I ask who sir is interviewing? Someone in the pop culture world?' I realized what was coming next and that I was falling into a deep, dark hole: 'Nobody important, just some slushy "moon in June" songwriter. I've really gotta go.' The recording stopped.

I felt about as dumb as you can get. I grinned weakly at Paul. Thanks to the dope both of us started laughing.

'First question?' said Paul, giggling.

'What rhymes with Moon?'

'June.'

'No Macca-roon.' (A pun on Paul's nickname.)

'That takes the biscuit.'

More hysterical laughter ...

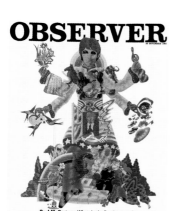

The interview with Paul McCartney lasted three hours and appeared first in the *Observer* magazine (26 November, 1967), then worldwide as 'The Beatles Sinister Songbook'. Left and opposite *Observer* cover illustration and detail.

Right Illustration to 'Got to Get You into My Life', done for *The Beatles Illustrated Lyrics*, 1969, but not published.

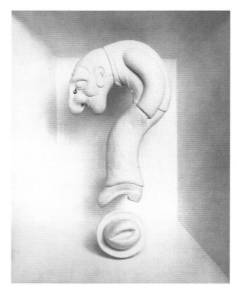

Illustrations for *The Beatles Illustrated Lyrics*, 1969.
Far left 'A Hard Day's Night'.
Left 'Nowhere Man'.
Below left Front cover.
Below 'Yellow Submarine'.
Far right 'Day Tripper'.

After illustrating the 'Beatles Sinister Songbook'
I had the idea for a more complete volume:
The Beatles Illustrated Lyrics was the result.
I approached seventy of the world's best
illustrators to contribute. What was left, or
what needed to be replaced because it was
too risqué to be published, I did myself.
I saw the book as an illustration of the sixties.

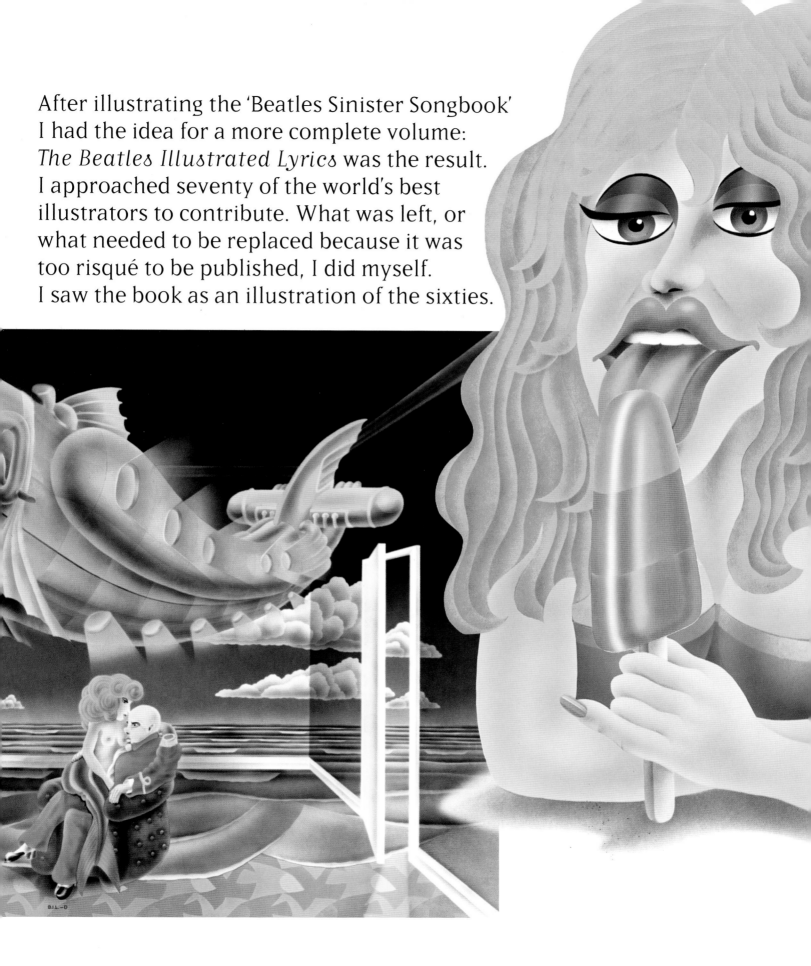

Illustrations for *The Beatles Illustrated Lyrics*, 1969.
Above 'Taxman'.
Opposite 'Sexy Sadie'.
Above right, top and bottom Outtakes from the 'Sexy Sadie' photo shoot.

Overleaf left and right Illustrations for *The Beatles Illustrated Lyrics*, 1969. 'Helter Skelter' and 'Tomorrow Never Knows'.

Illustrations for *The Beatles
Illustrated Lyrics*, 1969.
Opposite 'There's a Place'.
Above 'All You Need is Love'.
Right 'Yesterday'.
Below 'Revolution' by long-time
collaborator Harry Willock.

'Being for the Benefit of Mr Kite',
The Beatles Illustrated Lyrics, 1969.

Opposite Idea for a record player for
Apple Corps, 1969.

APPLE

Apple's first home was at 95 Wigmore Street: the place was dull, suitable for rheumatic accountants beset with colour blindness. I went there on a few occasions to do design jobs for Paul, primarily fine tuning the new Apple logo and EP holder. Paul had shown me a bunch of photos of red and green apples, which were being considered for Apple Corps Ltd, a company set up to help reduce the Beatles' tax bracket from 19s. 6d. in the pound to about 15 shillings. I suggested to Paul that he should use the green apple featured in a Magritte painting he owned which I'd seen at his house. The photo won out.

Then in autumn 1968 came 3 Savile Row – an old dowager of a building on a snotty street that would quickly become the centre of a psychedelic cyclone of deadbeats, dropouts and uncreative aspirants. The Lourdes of Freakdom.

My first visit was a bummer. I heard screaming, like angry cats, as I approached Savile Row and turning the corner from Vigo Street saw a melee of mostly teenage girls pushing and shoving around number 3's front door, yelling in their passionate agony for John, Paul, Ringo and George. I joined the throng and pushed my way through the mob. As the girls yelled and bayed I couldn't help noticing how bad British dentistry was. By the time I reached the front door I was roughed up real good: minus a few clumps of hair, with scratches on my face and an unknown jelly-like substance all over the back of my neck and T-shirt.

I banged on the door. It opened a crack. I yelled 'Derek Taylor' at a nervous eye and got yanked into the vestibule. The door was hastily slammed shut. Within weeks the hordes at the front door would change from pubescent British teens sporting knitted sweaters with Beatles' slogans to world-class con men: flunkies; junkies; and guys with secrets that tapped into the

ancient wisdoms for fuelless planes and death rays who were on the run from the FBI and the CIA. It became a mecca for the disenchanted: wordless poets and groupies from California, tanned and gorgeous beyond an Englishman's imagining; dropouts; unmusical musicians; jokeless comedians; musclemen; religious fanatics equipped with their own soapboxes; skinheads; Peeping Toms; peaceniks; and doom and gloomers, all wanting to sup on the mystical power of the Beatles.

Oh, yeah, one last character: George the Flower Man. George took a bunch of roses around the pubs of Soho, selling them off to drunk romantics at exorbitant prices. The unusual thing about George was that he had a water tap glued to his forehead. It was a brilliant marketing ploy for it got him lots of attention so that he could deliver his slobbery sales pitch. George discovered rich pickings at 3 Savile Row: people bought his roses and laid them at the front door with touching love notes.

Once inside, I went upstairs and met Derek Taylor, the Beatles press officer. You fell in love with this guy right away: warm, witty, urbane and full of hilarious repartee. Within minutes we were throwing jokes back and forth like ping-pong balls. I left with a couple of jobs.

After a couple of weeks, I called Derek and suggested he come over to INK, my studio on Litchfield Street, to take a look around. I wanted to show him that it had the potential to handle any amount of Apple design work. Derek arrived and got the 'bells and whistles' tour of the studio, stayed for a drink and declared on leaving that I was 'Design Consultan' (a pun, not a spelling mistake) to Apple.

For the next two years Derek and I saw a lot of each other and became friends. And it didn't rain work, it poured.

APPLE PORTABLE 45 rpm RECORD PLAYER

- DETACHABLE STEREO SPEAKERS
- BATTERY OPERATED
- HI - TONE STYLUS
- LIGHT WEIGHT
- VOLUME & TONE CONTROLS

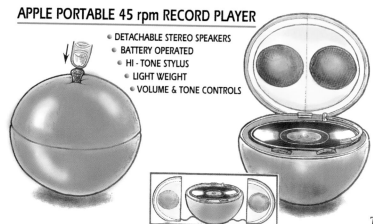

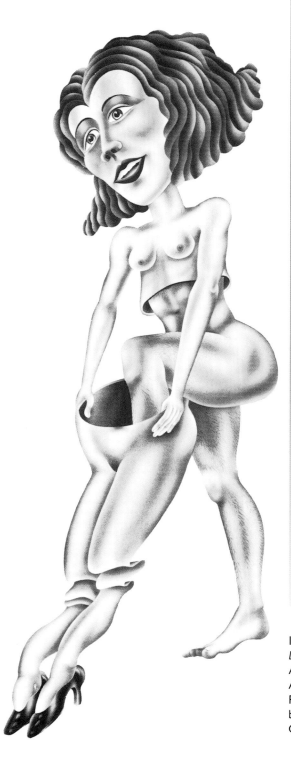

Illustrations for *The Beatles Illustrated Lyrics*, 1969.
Above left 'Get Back'.
Above 'Blue Jay Way'.
Right 'Dr Robert', this illustration was banned and published sometime later.
Opposite 'Cry Baby Cry'.

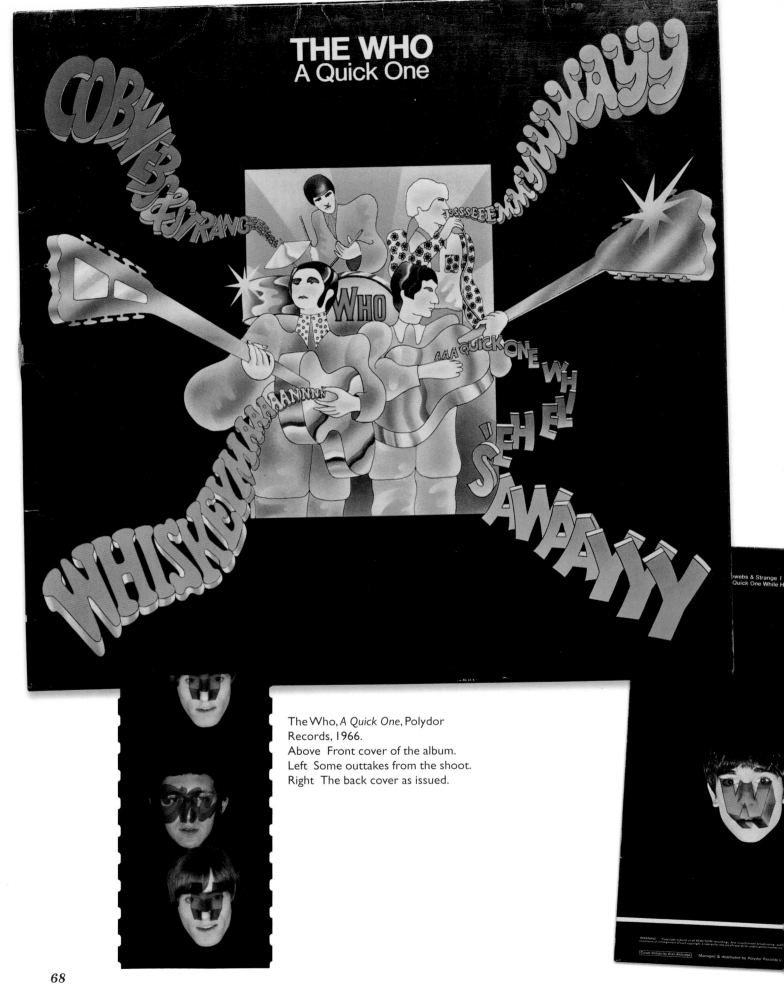

The Who, *A Quick One*, Polydor
Records, 1966.
Above Front cover of the album.
Left Some outtakes from the shoot.
Right The back cover as issued.

PINK FLOYD

I first saw Pink Floyd early in 1967 at the UFO club.

I'd heard 'Set the Controls for the Heart of the Sun' and couldn't stop humming it, perfect trippy music for a trippy time. I walked along the grey, rainswept streets of London to tacky Tottenham Court Road. A manky crowd of freaks in Afghan coats and bo-bo girls with huge mascaraed eyes loitered outside number 31, the UFO. I headed downstairs into a crowded basement where the beautiful people danced or sprawled on the floor, strobe lights and elasticated images of bubbles and breasts bombarded my eyeballs and for the first few seconds panicked the neurosignals to my cerebellum.

On stage four blokes struggled to hold some kind of free-form, other-worldly improvisation together; the low-grade amps were not doing the music any favours. The lead guitarist looked seriously out of it on something or other. He catawauled a mishmash of noises to twanging electronics that sounded like a cat getting neutered with a pair of blunt scissors.

It was Pink Floyd. I became an instant fan. I loved their audacity, their madcap improvisations, the apparent absence of structure in a pop world full of old-hat 'moon in June' music. They were catalysts for the coming revolution. I knew they'd be famous.

Two years later, I hired the 'boys' for £1,000 a night to do the soundtrack for an animated feature, *The Adventures of Rollo: The Boy Who Wasn't Who He Thought He Was*, which I'd created – another of those 'make me a millionaire' schemes which, through a series of unlikely events, didn't happen. I still have a 35mm reel of film. Probably worth a few bob …

Quick One Heatwave Run, Run, Run. So Sad About Us
Boris the Spider Don't Look Away

MONO 593 002

Right and overleaf *The Adventures of Rollo: The Boy Who Wasn't Who He Thought He Was*, 1969.
Film stills from the animated feature for which I asked Pink Floyd to do the soundtrack.

DALÍ

I'm sitting at the Bar Nuage at Nice airport in 1967. It's dawn and the place is empty. I'm on my fourth Alsatian beer; hair of the dog. I've just spent three days at the Hotel Metropole ooh la-la-ing with a famous French actress. She even picked up the tab, how good can life get?

As I wait for my BEA flight back to the Big Smoke I doodle dragons in the style of Utrillo on the pages of my copy of *The Hobbit*. A crowd enters, ten or twelve people yelling and screaming, their hands flying all over the place like demented pigeons. They swarm to the bar demanding espresso and brandy. I ignore being jostled, too hung over for 'bother' and continue sketching. Close behind me a man yells angrily in Spanish – he's definitely not ordering tapas; the crowd goes quiet. People snigger. Now he's ranting right in my ear, the stink of his breath makes me gag. The crowd laughs.

Maybe I'm getting the piss taken out of me so I swivel on my stool to face the joker and stare straight into the mad eyes of the King of Surrealists – Salvador Dalí. His head is cocked at a peculiar angle and he stares down his nose at me like an imperious cockerel, his pupils dilated pinheads. Dalí sprays spittle over me as incomprehensible words spew out. I demand a *parapluie* (umbrella) from the barman – the quip didn't get a laugh or produce an umbrella.

Dalí snatches the pen (a Waterman) from my hand, grabs *The Hobbit*, turns the page and begins rapidly sketching, blabbering a running commentary at the same time. It seems I'm getting a drawing lesson from the Master, but the only word I understand of the tirade is El Greco. Dalí scribbles at incredible speed, hand and pen blurring across the page. Magically, the tangled black lines turn into a rearing unicorn, gorgeously muscled. Dalí adds his quirky signature with an exaggerated flourish, then glares at me through the antennae of his famous moustache.

The crowd roars approval. Brandies are ordered. Dalí grins like the Cheshire Cat. He turns to a clean page then with slow deliberation pushes the book and pen back across the counter towards me. The egomaniacal bastard is challenging me to a drawing duel. The crowd tightens, Dalí's addled eyeballs bore through me. I stare at the page, my mind a blank. People snigger.

Dalí 71

Tenniel comes to my rescue; John Tenniel, illustrator of Lewis Carroll's *Alice* books and my hero. His picture of the Mad Hatter comes to mind – Dalí somehow looks like him. I start drawing, beginning with the top hat, adding the 10/6 ticket. The crowd cranes closer as I model the profile with its familiar hooked nose and protruding teeth. People nod and smile as they appear to recognize the Mad Hatter. I draw the huge, spotted bow tie, finally adding his ridiculous whiskers. It's a cheap shot but it gets a big, if short-lived, laugh.

Dalí is not amused. His mustachios vibrate with anger as his bloodshot eyes swell to saucers. He slams his malacca cane on the bar and snatches back the pen and book. He sneers at my drawing and makes an obscene gesture. Dalí finds a clean page and begins furiously to scribble a dense and erratic scrawl of lines, which rapidly and magically reveal a winged dragon. He ignores the crowd's applause and continues his frenetic assault – lines spew across the double page until the confusion reveals an armoured knight astride a rearing horse plunging a lance into the heart of the dragon. The drawing is exquisite.

'Los dragon Saint George', sneers Dalí, just inches from my face, 'de Inglaterra.'

The crowd roars olés. The barman pours freebie shots of brandy. Dalí, his raging machismo restored, slowly pushes the pen and book back to me. He grins like a wolf at his prey. I pick up the pen, gall scalds into my mouth. Dalí's grin widens to a sickening leer. The PA system announces the departure of Iberia Airlines flight to Barcelona. The crowd groans. They drain their glasses and make a move to the exit. Jesus' Mother and Christ, I'm saved!

I'm not. Dalí thwacks the marble counter with his cane. The departing crowd halts. The King of the Surrealists snaps an order.

Several gofers sprint out to the aeroplane revving its engines on the tarmac to deliver the edict. The crowd files back to the bar. Oh no. Dalí has ordered the plane to wait. Dalí grimly taps the open book with his cane. Time to renew the duel. I doodle aimlessly, unsure that I can top the Mad Hatter. Dalí hovers, reading my hesitation as defeat. He laughs, he sneers, he rants; spittle dribbles from his pallid lips, his jowls bulge and deflate and his cold, cod-fish eyes well with tears. He looks like a fish out of water. Cod-fish Dalí.

I start by drawing a fish's tail. As I sketch, the body for some inexplicable reason metamorphoses from a fish to

the fuselage of the waiting Iberia aeroplane. I detail windows, add wings and engines. A hush falls over the bar. Dalí stares unblinking at the drawing. I sketch a caricature of Dalí as the nose of the plane. The onlookers snigger, but not Dalí. Now, for the finale, I add Dalí's preposterous moustache and complete the drawing with an over-exaggerated autograph, Salvador-style.

Silence. The crowd waits for Dalí's reaction. He smiles thinly. Everyone cheers. People hug me, offer congratulations.

The gofers return from the tarmac. They report to Dalí that the aeroplane's pilot, Captain Ruiz, regrets that he can no longer delay the flight. Do M. Dalí and his companions wish to board? Dalí mutters 'Si'. He embraces me without comment and strides from the bar followed by his coterie.

As I watch the Iberia plane taxi to the ruway my flight to London is called. I spread a bunch of francs on the bar to pay for my drinks, but the barman insists, 'On the house'. I pick up *The Hobbit* and head out to the waiting BEA Viscount back to London.

The copy of *The Hobbit* got lost years later in a fire at my LA studio.

Above In the Rolling Stones' office, c. 1968, with Mick Jagger.

I was selling them the poster idea for the *Rolling Stones Rock and Roll Circus*. A nice moment.

Left Poster for the ill-fated documentary, *The Rolling Stones Rock and Roll Circus*, 1968. The film was eventually issued in 1996.

CREAM

Take a look at the back cover of the *Goodbye Cream* album. Have you ever seen such a happy band of rock'n'rollers?

Fact is, they hated each other. Cream, rock'n'roll's first supergroup: Eric Clapton, Jack Bruce and Ginger Baker. I knew all of them.

I first met Eric with George Harrison at a dinner party at Derek Taylor's house. (Derek was one of the candidates for the title of the fifth Beatle – he was press officer at Apple Corps.) It was a tribal gathering of prodigious herbal and alcoholic consumpion.

Ginger would come up to my studio if he was prowling Soho looking for the tamborine man. One time, he got so angry talking about Jack Bruce he slammed his fist and arm up to the elbow through the studio's thin plaster wall. When he withdrew it we looked through the hole and on the other side saw the family next door having dinner, not looking the least bit startled, as if fists came crashing through their walls all the time.

Jack I found quiet, but he warmed up if we discussed lyrics and poetry.

Through talking with each of them I learned that the personal dynamics of the band teetered on outright hate, mostly Jack for Ginger and Ginger for Jack, with Eric stuck in the middle anxious to get out a.s.a.p. This band isn't gonna last much longer, I thought, and it didn't.

Cream, *Goodbye Cream*, Polydor Records, 1969.
Above Outtakes from the photo shoot by Roger Phillips for the front (top) and back (bottom) of the album.
Opposite The back cover.

In the autumn of 1968, I got a call from the band's manager, Robert Stigwood, asking if I'd do an album cover for *Goodbye Cream*. The title said it all.

I did three roughs: something psychedelic; another funereal; and weirdest of all, I got this stupid visual in my head of the three lads dressed in top hat and tails hoofing their goodbyes off the stage. I shipped the ideas over to Stigwood's office, confident that the visually excessive druggy drawing would get chosen.

Wrong.

Stigwood called. He liked the top hat and tails idea, so apparently did Ahmet Ertegun (head of Atlantic Records, Cream's US record label).

Of course, I hated that one.

Within an hour Ahmet called me from New York to reiterate his unequivical approval of the Cream chorus-line concept. But … I'd never get the boys together to do the shoot. He bet £100 I'd fail.

Okay, Ahmet, you're on.

Eric, Jack and Ginger were roughly my size so to get things rolling I asked my tailor, Geoff, to make three suits in a metallic silver material. Top hats, canes and shoes got silvered from a spray can. But how to get the three 'boys' who detested each other to do the shoot? Time was of the essence … deadlines were closing in. I booked Roger Phillips to do the photography. Now it was down to the wire.

I had an idea. I called each of the boys and told them that I was gonna shoot them seperately on different days then marry the shots together at a photographic retoucher's. Happy, happy joy from one and all.

On the day of the shoot I'd arranged for each of them to come to my studio at half-hour intervals.

As each one arrived I gave them a double shot of brandy, then had my secretary walk them round the corner to Shaftesbury Avenue to the photographer's studio. There we had three separate dressing rooms set up, music amped to the max, lots to drink and, most importantly, three attractive dressers to fit the suits. I'd told the girls to prolong the fittings until they heard me call the guys out into the studio. There would be trouble when the three

rock stars saw each other and realized that they had been conned. Would they do a moody, tear off the clothes and walk-out act or worse? Could I handle the drama?

Plus, fact was I hadn't a clue how to choreograph the guys dancing off the stage, which meant that the whole shoot could be a disaster. I headed over to Roger's studio trailing black clouds of doubt, dreading the session, convinced I'd lost the plot and the £100 to Ahmet. The paranoia of failure swept through me and the crowds on the pavement all seemed to be pointing at me and laughing. All I wanted was a decent Christian burial.

Then, a miracle happened: a shining saviour was placed by the hand of God before me on the sullen streets of central London. My hero stood at the 38 bus stop. I wanted to kneel before him in supplication. It was Lionel Blair, king of London's theatrical stage dancers, TV celebrity, pantomime fairy. I saw a 38 bus coming. Gotta make this quick. I introduced myself and hurriedly explained my predicament: the band, the dance steps, the photographer waiting. The bus pulled to a halt. Lionel hesitated, half on half off the bus.

'On or off mate, make up your bleedin' mind,' barked the conductor.

'The band is Cream,' I yelled desperately as Lionel and the bus began to move off.

'Cream? Why didn't you say so, silly boy?' And he nimbly jumped from the bus. 'Oooh, I love them.'

We legged it to the studio. I banged on the doors of the dressing rooms. Out came Eric, Ginger and Jack resplendent one and all in their silver top hats and tails. In an instant they saw each other and in that split second Lionel, master of ceremonies and inflated egos, took over. Clapping, he yelled:

'Now girls, stop pulling faces, don't give me any moodies, come on, get in a line. Don't be frightened, squeeze in tighter, don't get too excited boys …'

Roger began shooting. Lionel, bless him, worked miracles, and for the next hour he had Cream doing the soft-shoe shuffle like pros.

Of course, all this had nothing to do with rock'n'roll but that's show buisness. As for the £100 bet, I never did get round to collecting it. At 8 per cent compound interest it would now be worth £1724.28.

CHELSEA GIRLS

It all started with a phone call from the Arts Lab.

The Arts Lab was in Covent Garden just around the corner from my studio. The place was a sanctuary for dropouts and pseudo-intellectuals spouting off about the coming apocalypse. You had Crowley freaks with inverted crosses tattooed on their foreheads and drop-dead gorgeous dolly birds looking for a 'fix' of one kind or another. John and Yoko went there maybe two or three times – we shared jokes over bowls of leaden macrobiotic rice.

Andy Warhol's *Chelsea Girls* movie was having its London premiere at the Arts Lab, which was a big deal, and Andy had asked if they could get me to do the poster. I didn't know anything about the movie, didn't want to, but this image hit me: a nude as the Chelsea Hotel with windows on the various floors open like an advent calendar to show all kinds of kinky perversions. The idea's genesis probably came from designing the cover for a new Beatles' album called *Dolls-house* (later to become the *White Album*, which I would also work on). That was to have been a picture of a doll's house with windows which opened to reveal a much darker and sordid interior.

I needed a model and a photographer. We would build the louvred windows, Plasticine figures and front entrance at INK Studios. I was fabulously lucky with the model. Her name was Clare Shenstone, a young art student. She was Cheddar-gorgeous!

This is how Clare remembers it:

My friend Calvin Lee, who was David Bowie's manager at the time, rang me and said that he had recommended me to Alan Aldridge as perfect for his poster idea. He hoped I would not mind. Alan, whom I had never met before, then rang and asked if I could come to his studio.

I remember walking the seven minutes from my flat to Alan's studio at Cambridge Circus.

'What does it involve?', I asked.

'I'm doing a poster for the British release of Chelsea Girls. *I want to make a hotel out of you. I need you nude for the shot but I will put windows and a door on you so bits are covered up in the final image. But I need to start with you nude. You can wear a jockstrap if you like but it would be much easier for me if you didn't.'*

I was thinking, what shall I do?

Alan added: 'I really need to get this shot done. Could I see your breasts? I haven't any money, so I can give you only fifty quid. Will you do it?'

Surprise, surprise, no money — but it didn't make much difference. If I was going to do it, it was because I liked the idea behind it. I rated the people involved very highly. I found myself suddenly confronted with whether I would do this one-off project, because I'd never agreed to do anything nude before, and later, when Tony Richardson tried to persuade me to play a part in his production of I, Claudius, *I refused because I would not do the nudity thing again.*

I met Don Silverstein for a drink. Don was an American photographer working in London. I liked his work, particularly his black-and-white pictures. I didn't show him a sketch of the poster, just told him I needed a 'contrasty' shot of a pretty girl posing nude for a film poster I was art directing for the Arts Lab.

'What's the fee?' he asked.

'There isn't one,' I answered. 'It's a "freebie", Arts Lab doesn't have any money.' He was cool …

'I'll do the pic if you cover my expenses.'

'What expenses?' I replied.

'I'll get the model. She'll need paying,' he said.

'I already have the model.'

'Then we'll need a hair stylist and make-up artist.'

'I'm doing the hair and the make-up.'

Don sussed that there was no money. He agreed to do the shoot anyway. A date was set for early evening at his studio.

I remember Don Silverstein's studio was comfortingly dark, but cold. Alan made up my face and they put a fire on to keep me warm; it was too close and too hot, but I did not say anything.

'Have you got a jockstrap like you said you would get me, Alan?'

'No, sorry, I didn't have time.'

Of course not, I'm thinking.

Not long afterwards, Alan rang and told me to come over to his studio.

'I've got the photograph — it's great, you must see it.'

designed by Alan Aldridge produced at ink Studios photography Donald Silverstein and Tempo printed by Charles Christopher Press

for the first time in this country in
its original continuous version running
for 3½ hours on two screens uncut

Andy Warhol's

Chelsea Girls

Oct 16th-19th (Wed-Sat) 23rd-26th (Wed-Sat)
7.00 pm till 12.00 midnight tickets 10/- (Bookable) 7/6
Arts Laboratory 182 Drury Lane WC2. 242-3407/8

'Are you happy with it?' I asked Alan.
'Absolutely.'

I went running down the road and
up the stairs to Alan's studio. There
were people everywhere, all standing
around, all looking down at something.
There was a gigantic blow up of me,
totally nude, lying on the floor. It was
beautiful when it was not of me, but
then it was me! All these people, who
the hell were they?

I said to Alan, 'For God's sake, cover
it up.'

'Don't you like it?' he asked.

'Yes, it's superb, but can't you cover
it up?'

A week or so later, I was with my
mother at Piccadilly Circus and saw
Alan by chance. He was waving and
holding something. I left my mother
and rushed over.

'Look,' he said, 'I've got the poster.
I just showed it to Paul McCartney and
he wants to meet you.'

'Don't get it out here, my mother
may see it!'

Today, my son and daughter
complain about having to deal with
their teachers and friends seeing an
image of their mother, nude, on the
Internet, but I have never had one
second of regret. I chose to do it,
and the poster is utterly superb.

The artwork was harder to get
printed than all the work to create it.
Every printer I called turned the job
down saying it could be deemed
pornographic. Finally, I called a friend
of mine who dealt in under-the-counter
porn who said that printing would be
no problem!

Soon the *Chelsea Girls* poster was
fly-posted all over the West End;
people's reaction to it was mostly shock.

Then I got a call from the Arts Lab.
Two policemen were looking for me;
they had a warrant for my arrest on
charges of distributing pornography.
My lawyer called the police. He was
informed by a detective that nipples
were not allowed to be exposed on
publicly displayed posters so I would
be charged under the Obscenity Act.
The lawyer told the officer that
I had not flyposted any posters and
had no control over how the Arts Lab
distributed them. The case was dropped.

Left *Chelsea Girls* poster, 1968.

Overleaf Posters for a concert by Led
Zeppelin and others, Roundhouse, London,
1968; and Holland Pop Festival, 1970.

Chelsea Girls **77**

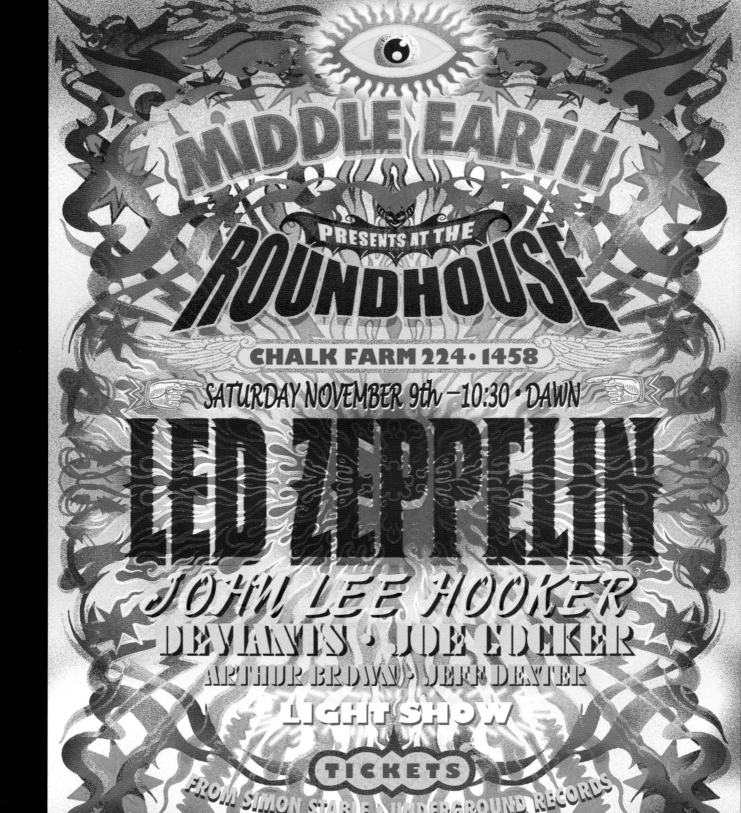

MIDDLE EARTH

PRESENTS AT THE

ROUNDHOUSE

CHALK FARM 224·1458

SATURDAY NOVEMBER 9th — 10:30 · DAWN

LED ZEPPELIN

JOHN LEE HOOKER

DEVIANTS · JOE COCKER

ARTHUR BROWN · JEFF DEXTER

LIGHT SHOW

TICKETS

FROM SIMON STABLE · UNDERGROUND RECORDS
207 PORTOBELLO ROAD
TOWN RECORDS KINGS ROAD

MEMBERSHIP 5/.

HOLLAND
POP FESTIVAL

26·27·28 JUNE 1970

BYRDS, THE CARAVAN, THIRD EAR BAND, INCREDIBLE STRING BAND, FAMILY, TYRANNOSAURUS REX, JEFFERSON AIRPLANE, JOHN SURMAN, PENTANGLE, PINK FLOYD, QUINTESSENCE, RENAISSANCE, SANTANA, SOFT MACHINE **ROTTERDAM** CHICAGO ART ENSEMBLE, EAST OF EDEN

Opposite On 18 May 1970, the day Harold Wilson called a general election for 18 June, the Labour Party's campaign poster was unveiled to journalists. The Conservative Party leaders caricatured were, from left to right, Iain Macleod, Enoch Powell, Edward Heath, Reginald Maudling, Quintin Hogg and Sir Alec Douglas-Home.

Below *Sunday Times* magazine, 14 June 1970, drawing by Burton Silverman, showing Alan Aldridge (far right, third from front) with other visitors to 10 Downing Street during the Wilson government.

In the spring of 1970, the Prime Minister, Harold Wilson, called me with an urgent commission – could I do a *trompe l'oeil* painting in the dining room at 10 Downing Street in preparation for a formal dinner with the Pope. The subject should be a bacchanalia in the style of Caravaggio and the honeyed chiaroscuro of Georges de La Tour, with Edward Heath (Leader of the Opposition) as Bacchus guzzling wine, lots of fairies being ravished by the cast of Carry on Camping, members of the royal family, drunken dwarves, etc. As an added filip the Prime Minister said that if I did a good job I'd be mentioned in the next Honours List ... mmm, I thought, Sir Alan Aldridge, rolls off the tongue real easy. Except it didn't happen – I was just kidding you!

However, I did get a call from KMP (Kingsley Manton and Palmer), a hip advertising agency, asking me to attend a meeting at Downing Street. It was to discuss a poster campaign for the upcoming General Election and was to be chaired by Harold Wilson. The Labour Party was odds-on favourite to be re-elected.

At Number 10 I met the Prime Minister and the team of PR and advertising specialists from KMP. I was asked to design a poster campaign called 'Yesterday's Men'. They wanted to show the Conservative Party Shadow Cabinet led by Ted Heath as tired, out of date old men, but with the proviso that I was not to do anything too cartooney or grotesque.

A week later I'd done sketches of Heath and his closest colleagues, seven men in all, including Enoch Powell who was no longer in the Shadow Cabinet but whose presence might gain the Labour Party a few extra votes because of his controversial views on immigration. The figures were realistic and would be modelled as three-dimensional caricatures in Plasticine. Wilson and the KMP team gave me the go-ahead. The figures got made and photographed.

I collected the 5 x 4" transparencies from the photographer's studio. They looked great. The ad agency people raved and asked me to take them over to Downing Street. I got to Number 10 and told the policeman at the front door that I had an appointment with the Prime Minister. He gave me one of those 'What the hell could a long-haired git dressed like a pansy out of a pantomime be doing with the Prime Minister' down his nose looks that British bobbies practise for months to perfect. Fortunately, before we got into a contretemps, the front door opened and the Prime Minister's political secretary, Marcia Williams, ushered a visitor out, saw me and invited me in. She escorted me through to the library. The Prime Minister was relaxing in a comfy armchair and greeted me warmly. He offered an armchair, so I sat down.

'So, how are the photos, young man?' Nothing about the weather, just straight to the point. I pulled the transparencies from a bag and held them up one at a time against the light of the lamp on the table between us. He hummed and ha'd, in between mumbling, 'Yes ... good ... good ... mmmm' and seemed genuinely astonished at how beautiful the pictures were.

'Excellent job, young man. Nothing on my agenda, time to relax with a cigar. Care to join me?'

He opened an ornate box and offered me a cigar: each one was wrapped in tissue paper on which was printed 'Handmade for the Right Honourable Harold Wilson'. The band said Royal Jamaica and curiously they were Churchill-size cigars, made popular by a previous prime minister. I was a cigar

WHEN ALL THE BEAUTIFUL PEOPLE CAME TO THE AID OF THE PARTY

aficionado, Montecristo's being my smoke of choice. I took the cigar, rolled it between my fingers, listening to the moisture content of the wrapper. It was perfect. Harold passed me cigar cutters. I positioned them on the cap of the cigar and with a quick snip and a clean cut I was ready to light up.

I put the cigar in my mouth and gently enjoyed that meditative pleasure of savouring the first delicious musky flavours of the languid smoke. We sat in silence for several minutes, drawing on our cigars and blowing smoke, both smiling at the pleasure of the moment.

'Aldridge, do you taste the robust, bitter flavour of espresso?'

'More like mocha for me, with just a hint of cherry,' I replied.

'Mmm, now as the cigar reveals itself I'm getting a creamy nutmeg and anise taste, wonderful.'

'I'm sensing an aroma of woody earth and a soupçon of roast chestnuts.'

'Indeed, Aldridge, pistachio too and subtle notes of nutmeg and and cedarwood.'

'The woody aroma is fresh-turned earth – by a fork not a tractor, Sir.'

'Perceptive, young Aldridge.'

Finally, I said to Harold, 'Sir, I got the impression you were strictly a pipeman?'

The Prime Minister drew on his cigar, let the smoke unfurl over his palette then opened his mouth and let the tangled ropes of smoke curl gently up to the ceiling.

'Aldridge, the pipe is for the proletariat.'

I wasn't sure if I was supposed to laugh, but I did ... proletariat indeed. Politicians, con men, one and all.

The 'Yesterday's Men (They failed before!)' posters went up all over Britain. A furore ensued and the Conservatives and many newspapers called it the worst smear campaign

in the history of British politics. The Labour Party and Wilson unexpectedly lost the election.

Below **With the Plasticine models made for the poster. The model of Sir Keith Joseph, second from right, was not used.**

OBSERVER CHILDREN'S BOOKS

6 DECEMBER 1970

DISCOVERING A LOST WONDERLAND

Alan Aldridge illustrates a remarkable fantasy rescued after 40 years in a junk box – page 15.

Frances D. Francis was a 72-year-old lady who lived in the Queen's Head, a genteel hotel in Minehead, Somerset. She'd written *Ann in the Moon* in 1928 when she was thirty for her housekeeper's granddaughter and some forty years later had found the manuscript in an old trunk. Bancroft (part of BPC Publishing) asked if I'd be interested in illustrating the story. I read it and liked it and worked around the clock to do as many drawings as I could in the six-week schedule. I was commissioned to do four but in the end produced more than twenty.

Above *Observer* magazine, 6 December 1970. **Discussing the illustrations with Mrs Francis in the hotel room that was her home.**

Below The front cover of *Ann in the Moon* by Frances D. Francis and Alan Aldridge, published by Bancroft, London, 1970.

Illustrations from *Ann in the Moon* and (top) title page.

Overleaf A spread from the book and, on page 88, a further illustration.

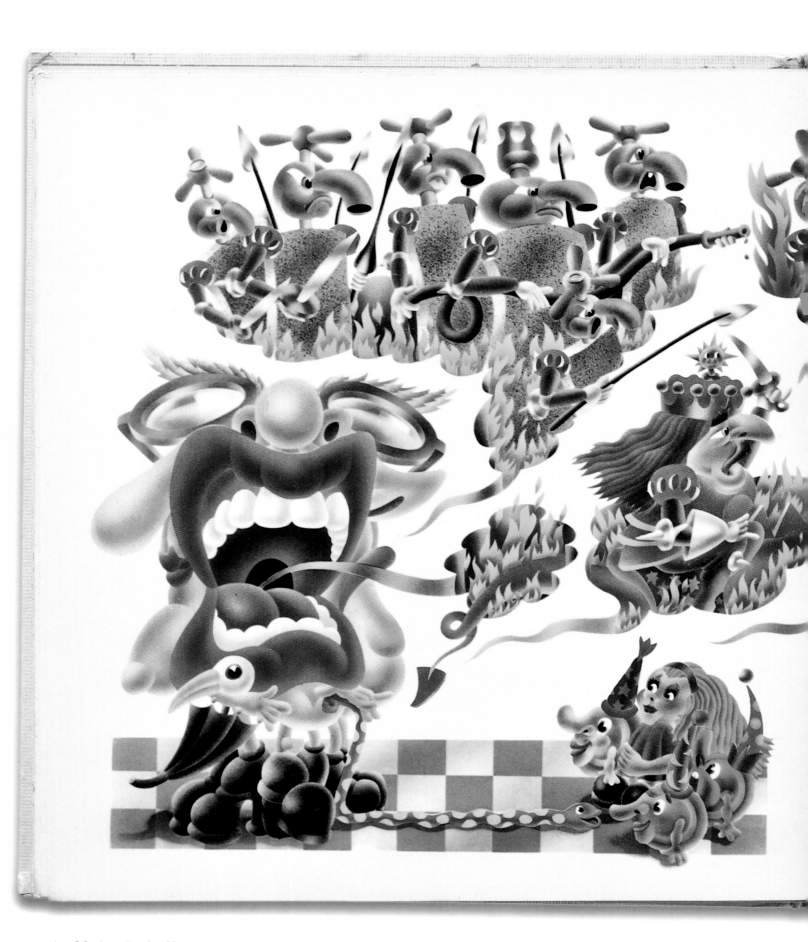

And the eight Sunkins were so frightened at what might happen next that they jumped clean off their piece of Sun and disappeared into nowhere. This so upset Moondial and his wife that they kissed and made it up and settled down to feel very unhappy at the loss of their children. In fact, they were so unhappy that they forgot to feel cross or frightened any more.

"When we stop falling I will bake you some more Sunkins," said So Fa Me Ray when they had cried for two days and two nights without stopping. This cheered Moondial up a lot, especially as he had remembered to bring the baking oven which Sun children are always baked in, just like nice new cakes. After that he started to feel happier.

In 1970, *The Beatles Illustrated Lyrics* book won me a big award in Japan. I was invited by the Japanese government to put on an exhibition of my work in Tokyo at the National Museum of Modern Art. To be honest, I wasn't too keen to go. I'd heard that the Japanese ate something called sushi – octopus, sea urchins and raw fish – didn't use knives and forks, that their beer was tasteless, the geisha girls were really men, nobody spoke English and they hated 'long noses' (westerners).

I flew BOAC, fourteen hours flying time with a four-hour stopover in Moscow. I buoyed up my lack of enthusiasm for the trip by drinking endless amounts of Johnnie Walker Black Label with ginger ale, consequently I arrived at Narita airport with a leaden hangover. I stepped from the aircraft and saw hordes of paparazzi pushing and shoving at the bottom of the steps. I hurried down thinking the jostling cameramen were waiting to shoot someone famous coming down behind me.

Surprise. When I hit the tarmac they surrounded me in a hyena-like frenzy, screaming, pushing and shoving, shooting off pictures, cameras clicking like angry toads. Finally, a 'chinless wonder' from the British Embassy pushed through the mob and bundled me into a waiting limo. Once hunkered in the back seat, 'Chinless' showed me a copy of the English language *Japan Times*. Front centre was a photo of me captioned 'World famous British artist to open his exhibition in Tokyo at Museum of Modern Art'. World famous? I doubt if anyone knew of me north of London's Camden Town.

We got to the hotel, The Imperial. There were more photographers and a twenty-man welcoming committee from the hotel, the museum and Seibu, a Japanese chain of department stores that was sponsoring the Aldridge exhibition. I spent the next couple of hours as if I was in a Charlie Chaplin movie, bowing and rebowing to each of the welcoming committee in turn with everyone handing me their business cards. I learnt my second Japanese word: 'Hi', spat out with military gusto. It means 'hello'. The only other Japanese word I knew was 'sayonara', which means goodbye, and is the title of a really bad Marlon Brando movie.

At last I got to my suite, went to the mini bar, had a night cap and fell into a dark dream of being a Japanese prisoner of war. At 6.30 a.m. the phone rang. I woke up humming the Colonel Bogey march from *Bridge Over the River Kwai*. Weird. I picked up the phone. A voice informed me that I had a breakfast meeting in the lobby at 7 a.m. Half an hour later I hit the lobby and not only were the same people there whom I'd met on my arrival, but another ten or more. We went through the same ritual bowing and rebowing as an interpreter explained who each person was, their titles and respective organizations. We were 'hi-ing' for close to an hour. Finally, I was introduced to Yoko, a young Japanese woman who would be my interpreter.

I discovered that the exhibition was to open the next day and various press interviews had been lined up, the most important being a TV appearance in a couple of hours' time on the biggest talk show in Japan. It aired live from ten to eleven o'clock five days a week and the whole of Japan – from housewives to factory workers, shipping tycoons to vending machine operators – took a tea break to watch it. Its audience was a staggering 20 million people, some 80 per cent of all TV owners in Japan. The president of Nippon TV (the network that it), a sour looking man, told me I would be asked by the talk-show host to do a drawing during the interview and to dedicate it to the Japanese people. I declined. Dashing off a drawing on live TV wasn't my kind of gig. The president, not used to refusals, glared at me as if I was a kamikaze pilot who refused to fly.

At last, we went for breakfast. The hotel dining room was sumptuous, the food less so. I was encouraged to have a traditional Japanese breakfast. It came on a tray, about ten small dishes, and the only thing I recognized was a dried up skeletal-looking kipper. Yoko explained the dishes to me: boiled rice, pickled vegetables, miso soup and nori – a paper-thin seaweed that had been used centuries ago to make glue and tasted like it.

After breakfast a fleet of limos raced our entourage to the network's studios. Prior to going on stage, I was primped and talculmed and then escorted to the Green Room where I downed a couple of cups of sake. I figured I was about to appear with someone like Michael Parkinson in front of an audience of about ten doddery old so and sos or maybe no audience at all. Finally, I got

the call to go on stage for the interview; Yoko followed, ready to interpret.

A stage assistant escorted me along a dark tunnel and I stepped on stage, fingered by spotlights. I blinked, squinted, blinked again. I couldn't believe my eyes. The TV studio was huge, an indoor stadium with people crowded on seats vaulting way up to the rafters, maybe 3,000, maybe a lot more. On stage was a thirty-piece orchestra. As I exited from the tunnel the musicians launched into a jazzy rendition of 'Hey Jude' and the crowd roared. Placed among the instrumentalists were lots of my paintings on artists' easels. Wow, this was a big production.

I got to the front of the stage and the assistant waved me towards the talk-show host, a benevolent grey-haired man standing on a low dais, empty except for two chairs. We bowed to each other. I held my hand out, he hesitated, looking puzzled, playing to the audience. Yoko said something in Japanese and his face beamed. He pumped my hand with way too much vigour but it got a big laugh from the adoring crowd. I began to think that the interview was going to be okay.

Then I saw an easel with a blank sheet of paper and a black pen next to the dais. I was going be asked to do a drawing. My mind went blank. A shiver of panic ran through me. This was bad news. It was about to get

worse. Without warning, the band went out of sync. Rapidly 'Hey Jude' became a dissonant catawaul. The audience was screaming. I was thinking, Is this some kind of joke? Pandemonium erupted. The band wailed into silence as the musicians abandoned their instruments and ran for the exits. The screaming got louder. The host looked panicked and dived to the floor.

I was still standing, totally bemused, but thinking this was the coolest interview I'd ever had. Something huge and dark was gliding just over my head, I felt the breeze of its wings. Suddenly I was scared. What the hell was that? A stagehand rugby tackled me, pulling me to the floor. Now I saw it, a winged creature. It was wheeling above me, curving in a tight circle, then plummeted towards me.

Beejazzers, it was an eagle.

But what the hell was an eagle with a six-foot wingspan doing flying around a TV studio? The eagle flew over me, so close I could have caught the jesses tied to its taloned feet. The beautiful bird sailed upward towards the roof. People were fighting to get out of the studio. I watched as the eagle gyrated gorgeously on its magnificent wings.

It hit the roof with a sickening smack. Feathers exploded and it dropped like a bundle of rags to the studio floor. It was exactly eleven o'clock. The show was over. The host stood shaking and

talking to me at ninety words a minute. Yoko said she'd translate in the car as we had to leave for my next interview ...

In the limo heading across town Yoko explained what had happened. Prior to me going on stage a fisherman was interviewed who had trained two eagles to catch fish in the bay of Tokyo. Not only to catch fish but also to bring them back to the fisherman in his boat, who would reward the birds with a piece of meat. He had brought two eagles to the studio to demonstrate their ability to pick up a fish and bring it to him. However, the clapping of the audience had spooked one of the eagles and it had flown up and perched in the rafters. With the attitude that the show must go on, I was wheeled out for my interview. The rest, as they say, is history. Except ...

The show's sensational events hit every TV channel in Japan; it was even suggested that I'd organized the whole thing as a stunt to attract people to my exhibition. It did. Next day, when I arrived at the museum to open the show, there were about 2,000 people waiting and everyone was talking about my appearance on the talk show – the exhibition became one of the most successful art shows ever held in Japan.

Opposite *The Artist as Goldfish Bowl* was used on the poster for the Tokyo exhibition, 1970.

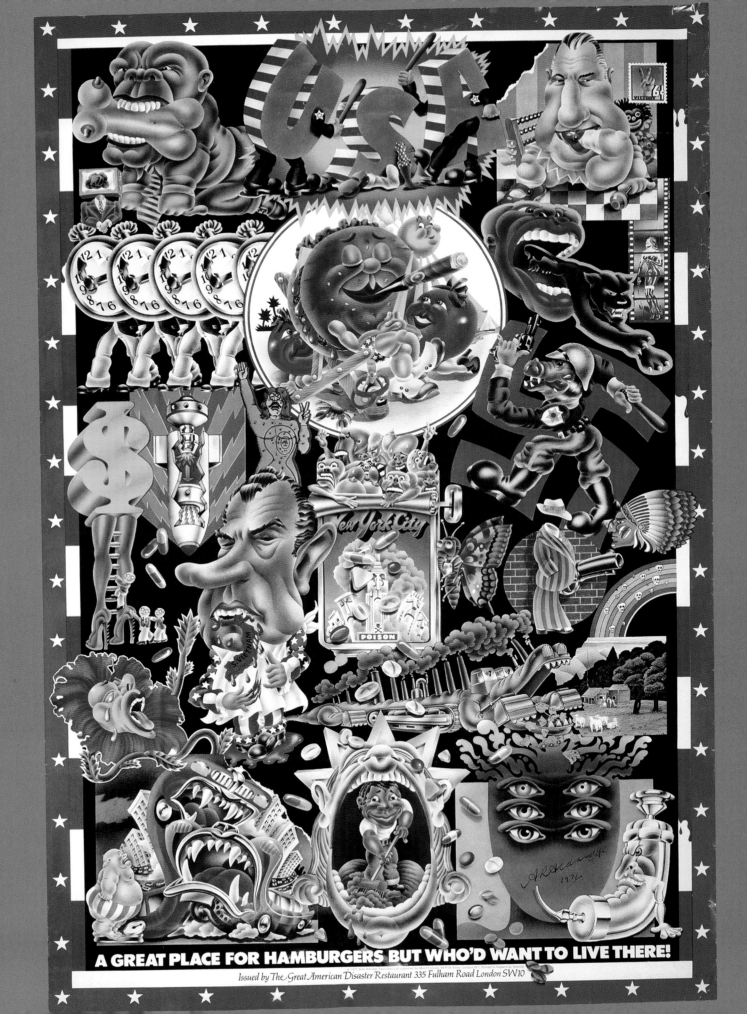

Opposite Poster for the Great American Disaster Restaurant, 335 Fulham Road, London, 1971.

Hard Rock Cafe. Below Logo, 1971; centre below and right 20th anniversary versions of the logo, 1991; bottom Architect's drawing of south elevation of the Hard Rock Hotel, Las Vegas. **I added a guitar to 'rock'n'roll' the austere exterior, 1994.**

SOUTH ELEVATION

The Butterfly Ball and the Grasshopper's
Feast by Alan Aldridge and William
Plomer, published by Jonathan Cape,
London, 1973.
Below 'Harlequin Hare', plate 5, and
original sketch.
Opposite Front cover.

By the early seventies the Beatles had broken up and I'd moved to a thirty-room rectory in Norfolk. Partly inspired by the success of *Ann in the Moon*, I wanted to take my time and create more illustrated children's books.

I made regular trips to the library at the British Museum, searching through Victorian children's books for something that appealed enough to spend several months illustrating it. I found it in *The Butterfly's Ball and the Grasshopper's Feast*, a poem by William Roscoe, published in 1807.

Inspired by the title (which I slightly altered) and characters, I worked for over a year until I had completed twenty-eight plates. Now I needed some new verses (the original ones were a bit dated). I approached W. H. Auden but after a few weeks of yes-ing and no-ing he turned me down. Next was Sir John Betjeman, who no-ed and yes-ed, finally yes-ed, then didn't write anything. By this time I'd done a deal with Jonathan Cape and they planned to publish the book in September 1973. So the poet William Plomer (who was also literary adviser at Cape) was given about four weeks to write the verses. Thanks to a brilliant piece in the *Sunday Times* magazine, it became a huge hit, selling 100,000 copies by Christmas 1973 and going on to be the biggest selling children's illustrated book in the world.

THE Butterfly BALL AND THE GRASSHOPPER'S FEAST

Alan Aldridge & William Plomer

Original sketch and the final artwork for
'Homeward', plate 28.

Opposite Original sketch and the final
artwork for 'Waiting for a Bite', plate 18.

And there close by the bank
Mr Fisher gives a grin

Although he'd caught no fish since mornings first light
Mr Fisher smiled at poor Grasshoppers plight —
Then with keen eyes search the muddy stream for fish
To take home and cook with berries, mm a delicious dish

CAN YOU FIND A FISH

Original sketches and the final artwork
for 'Magician Moth', plate 9.

'Harold the Herald', plate 1.

'Major Nathaniel Gnat', plate 7.

CAPTAIN FANTASTIC

Part 1 The Album

The avuncular Dick James was the luckiest man in show business. He hit a mega-mega cash-cow jackpot not once, but twice. In early 1963, Dick signed the not yet super-famous Beatles to his music publishing company, Dick James Music (DJM). Then in 1968 he employed a chubby, four-eyed teenager, Reg Dwight, as a gofer to write songs and make tea in his Denmark Street studio. Reg Dwight would metamorphose into Elton Hercules John and become the world's number one entertainer during the 1970s – and Dick owned a major pound of flesh of Elton's songs.

In the spring of 1975, Dick phoned me in Norfolk asking if I'd come to a meeting in London with him and Bernie Taupin, author of all Elton's lyrics, but I would have to wear a tie! Suitably dressed, we met at the Sportsman club on Tottenham Court Road. Elton and Bernie wanted me to design Elton's next album. I took a *Captain Fantastic* tape back home. I'd expected something like 'Crocodile Rock' or 'Saturday Night's Alright (For Fighting)' but the songs were dark, brooding, suicidal. A Boschian view of life on the rock'n'roll road to Hell. I drew a cover showing a quagmire of pimps and con men, thieves and despots, rats, poseurs, losers and boozers, all trying to grab a piece of Captain Fantastic. During the execution of the artwork I broke my thumb playing soccer for Foulsham, the local village team, which is why on the album liner notes Elton's dedication reads: 'For Alan Aldridge, his thumb and imagination.'

This is Elton's recollection: Captain Fantastic and the Brown Dirt Cowboy *was a milestone album for Bernie and me in so many ways. It was released in May 1975 and became the first album ever to enter the Billboard album chart at number one, was certified Platinum (a million copies) on its first day, and stayed at number one for seven weeks.*

The album is autobiographical and, as Bernie said, was about the dark side of Tin Pan Alley. Weeks before its release we had met up with Alan Aldridge, whom we knew as one of the leading pop artists of the sixties and seventies. We had a brief meeting — I was heading off to America — and we tried to explain what the album was about. Alan seemed to grasp straight away that there was a dark and surreal side to these songs. Bernie gave him a cassette and off we went, leaving Alan with complete artistic freedom to design the album art in about three weeks.

The finished picture was quite small — smaller than the gatefold sleeve of the record — but minutely detailed, airbrushed, fascinating. We loved it. Alan had captured the heart of the album better than we could have ever hoped. It has always been one of my favourite album sleeves. Alan received a Grammy nomination for it — I think he deserved the full award.'

But I was excited by something much more than the album cover. Captain Fantastic was a catchy name and with the world's number one pop star attached you had the basic ingredients for a major animated movie. I started scribbling ideas about the adventures of Captain Fantastic (Elton), a city boy, and The Kid (Bernie), a country bumpkin, two wannabee rock stars who meet up

and set off down the Yellow Brick Road to mythical Poptropolis, city of rock'n'roll dreams (and nightmares), in a quest to meet the King of Rock'n'Roll.

I wrote a rough film treatment and arranged to see John Reid, Elton's manager. When I got to his office I was surprised to find Bernie and Elton there too. I showed my presentation, laying the drawings out on the carpet and giving a running commentary of the plot. They loved it.

John Reid said he'd set up a meeting with Sid Sheinberg, president of Universal Pictures, the movie arm of MCA, Elton's music distributors. I flew to LA and John Reid and I met Sheinberg. I pitched the movie using little cut-out figures of the characters, standing them on his desk as I did my spiel, going through the basic plot. When I'd finished, Sheinberg looked at John and simply said, 'What d'you need to get this made?'

John responded, 'A monthly allowance for Alan, a house on Barbados for three months for Bernie and Alan to write the script, and an office in Beverly Hills.' He got everything he asked for.

It became a two-year gig of every excess: booze, drugs, sex and penury.

Opposite Proof of the backglass design for the *Captain Fantastic* home pinball machine made by Bally, 1977.

Above Elton John, *Captain Fantastic and the Brown Dirt Cowboy*. Album cover design and illustration by Alan Aldridge / Harry Willock with lettering help from Geoff Halpin at Bloomsbury Group, DJM Records, 1975.

Right The record label, 1975.

Overleaf Detail of the 20 x 30" fold-out poster that came with the album.

Captain Fantastic and the Brown Dirt Cowboy, sketches for animated film characters and one of the scenes (overleaf left), and poster for the proposed film (overleaf right), 1977.

Part 2 The Movie

In 1976 I was to join Bernie in Barbados to write the first draft of the script. Universal had provided us with a big old plantation house on posh Sandy Lane. The place had bedrooms aplenty and at least six live-in servants. Bernie and I arrived lacerated by marriages gone bad, and were more interested in drowning our sorrows at a night club called Joseph's than sitting around developing a script.

I was on my way out the first evening when I found the staff lined up in the entrance hall. A middle-aged lady stepped forward and said something which I didn't understand. She showed me sheets of paper covered in loopy handwriting. I was unable to read the writing but nodded an okay.

The following evening as we left about nine for another session at Joseph's I noticed the staff were

standing formally around the beautifully set dining table laden with dishes heaped with salads and cuts of meat. This went on for three or four days, until the middle-aged lady came to see me. She was upset. She explained that on my first evening she had presented me with the dinner menus for the week which I had approved. Consequently the chef had prepared meals for us and our guests every night, and every night no one had shown up. I apologized profusely. Bernie and I had dinner at the house for the rest of our stay – which wasn't long …

One afternoon, Bernie and I, accompanied by Oliver Reed, the English actor and the nicest reprobate, who was holidaying on Barbados, went to a tin-shack tacky bar on the edge of a sugar-cane field. It was definitely a joint for the locals – you could feel the hostility as soon as we walked in. We ordered Banks Beer, a local brew, and sat at a

table telling jokes, minding our own business. A couple of beers later, three weed-smoking Rasta dudes approached us. After some non-threatening jive talk about how white boys ought not to stray too far from the beach, they challenged us to a rum-drinking contest. We didn't want to appear wimpy, so we agreed. They explained the rules: the team that drank the most shots would win. The prize was US$50.

Both teams put their money on the table. Everyone in the bar crowded around the table. The barman brought lots of shot glasses to the table – as you popped a shot your glass was put on a tin tray to record your team's total score. We did shots in turn. When a Barbadian downed his shot the crowd cheered and chanted 'Nya-binghy-nya-binghy', when one of us did a shot the place erupted in boos and catcalls.

By my sixth shot I was feeling decidedly green at the gills and dropped

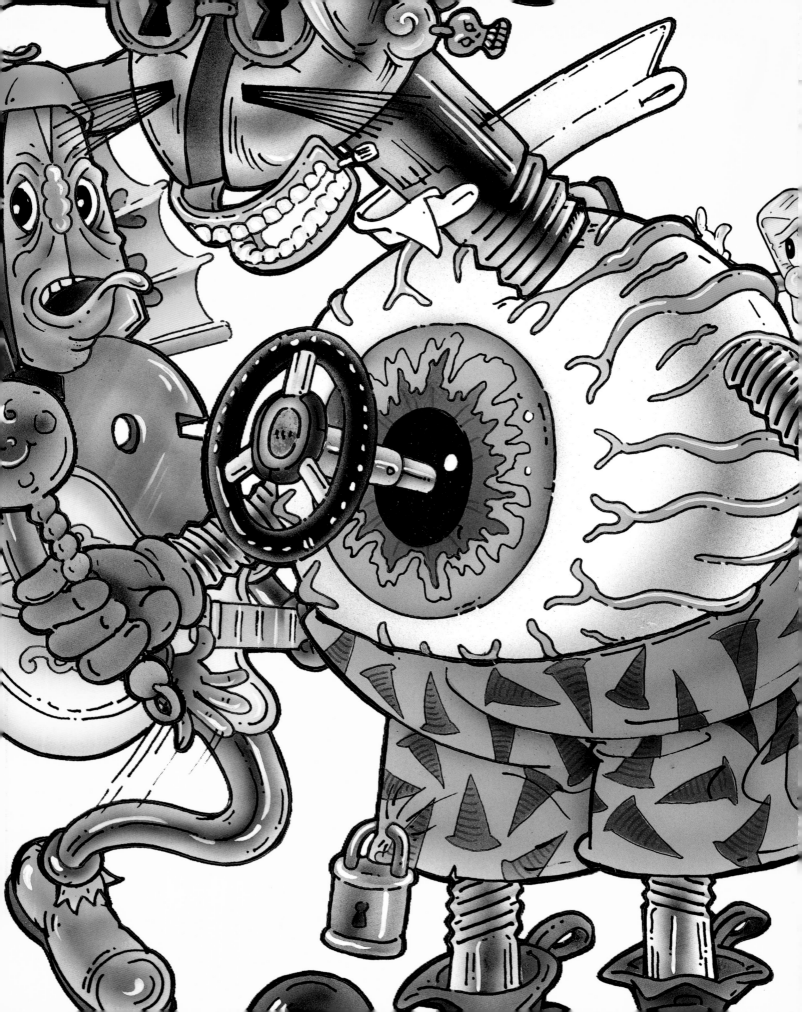

out; Bernie was next at eight. The score stood at England 22, Barbados (with all three of their team still in) 24. Oliver did his ninth shot and finally one of the Barbadians crashed out. Oliver knocked back ten and eleven and another Barbadian stumbled on his tenth. England 25, Barbados 28.

On the thirteenth shot the last of the Barbados team passed out, which left Oliver needing to pop four more shots to win. The bar went quiet as Oliver, who seemed totally in control of his faculties, blithley downed four shots and said 'Gentlemen, I think that's a win for England.' He scooped up the money, then threw it back on the table and yelled, 'Barman – drinks all round'. The place exploded with appreciation.

I don't remember leaving the bar or much of the next couple of days as I weaved in and out of alcoholic delirium – I finally surfaced with a massive headache and found Bernie in similar straits. We decided Barbados was a bad idea as far as working was concerned; it was time to skedaddle and head for LA.

We went to say goodbye to Oliver at his hotel – but were told he'd been asleep for the past two days and didn't look like waking anytime soon. We were glad he was still alive …

LA was different – it's Tinseltown, the movie capital of the world. There's an energy about the place, a dog eats dog, sink or swim, that energizes you to wanna work, and work we did.

Captain Fantastic Enterprises had an office on South Beverly Drive where Bernie and I had desks facing each other. We'd get in around noon each day and I would talk through each unfolding scene and Bernie would type away adding his own ideas – in less than eight weeks we had a draft script done. Universal loved it and the initial budget we worked out with an animation studio … things were rockin' … surely the project was unstoppable?

There was also the merchandising. I flew to New York to meet Stan Lee, head of Marvel Comics – he too fell in love with the Captain and we got an agreement to do twenty-six

monthly issues of *Captain Fantastic's Adventures in Poptropolis*.

Next, there was a meeting at the Four Seasons restaurant with the legendary merchandising agent Ed Justin. I liked Ed, a lugubrious, world-weary sort of a guy who cracked jokes without creasing a smile. He wanted exclusive world rights to represent Captain Fantastic – he was so sure the project would make millions that he was prepared to put up his own money. Ed withdrew from the inside pocket of his overly tight Brooks Brothers suit what looked like a solid gold cigarette case, rectangular in shape. What happened next goes down in my annals of 'memorable moments'. He placed the case on the table, not saying a word. For about fifteen seconds it just sat there, then the top half opened and swung in an arc until each half lay side by side like an open book. A lid opened slowly on the left side and a chequebook slid out on a gold tray; on the right another lid opened and a solid gold pen emerged, cocked upwards ready for use.

'I'll write you guys [referring to Elton, Bernie, John Reid and myself as owners of Captain Fantastic Enterprises] an open cheque.' Ed picked up the pen ready to write a number. I was impressed, but ...

'Ed, you need to talk to John Reid. He handles all that stuff.'

After that I went back to the Plaza Hotel for a meeting with an executive from Bally, one of the world's leading gaming manufacturing companies. We'd done a deal with them to make a pinball machine to tie in with the film. He had flown from Chicago to show me some artwork that their studio had done. I was excited – this would be the first evidence that the project was becoming a reality. I met Tom Neiman in the Oak Room and after some chitchat he pulled out a large board from a bag:

'This is the art for the backglass, hope you like it.'

I didn't! Captain Fantastic and the Brown Dirt Cowboy looked awkward and goofy. I told Tom as politely as

I could that the picture wasn't right. He thought for a moment.

'Alan, could you come to Chicago?'

Two weeks later I was there. Designing a pinball machine for Bally was a dream commission. My house in Norfolk was like a pinball arcade with the machines I'd collected since I'd started making a bit of money.

The intricacies were explained to me by 'Norwegian' Dave Christianson, Bally's star artist. Over the next week I drew up all aspects of the machine as fast as I could. The backglass art was sent to Harry Willock in London for his masterly airbrush colouring; pencil drawings for the playfield and wooden body got distributed to various artists in the Bally studio.

Six months later I was at my house in Norfolk and heard someone banging at the front door. A huge wooden crate was being delivered – funny, I hadn't ordered anything. I bust open the crate and there it was: the Captain Fantastic pinball machine, a thing of true beauty. I still have it ... somewhere!

While I was working on the film, Universal put me in the Beverly Wilshire Hotel, just around the corner from the office. My suite was on the same floor as Warren Beatty's. Most nights, after cavorting around town checking out the 'scene', I'd go back to the hotel and head for the dark, nightclub ambience of the El Padrino Room, find a seat at the bar and enjoy a drink. El Padrino wasn't some hole-in-the-wall dive open to passing stumblebums, but a fancy nightspot for the well heeled, inside one of America's top hotels. So when this guy started to come into the bar with matted beard and hair detonating out of his head in every direction I thought it odd that he wasn't given the bum's rush from the place. He never spoke, not even to get served, same drink every night – if I remember right, Chivas with water – placed in front of him the second he bellied up to the bar.

After a couple of weeks of him coming in and the two of us eyeballing each other and not saying a word, he spoke. I was headed to the 'john'

Scene
design (left)
and Poptropolis
(above) for proposed
animated film, 1977.

and as I walked past him, he said:

'You gotta a Triumph mo'sickle?'

'Ugh?'

He pointed to my lapel, where I had an enamel badge of the Triumph motorcycle company logo.

'Nah! Just the badge. Less dangerous.' I moved on to the men's room.

At the urinal I decided I'd give the hairy old bum a few laughs with a couple of motorcycle jokes, but when I got back to the bar he'd gone. The next night, I showed up at eleven o'clock and there was Mr Hirsute Head already downing his Chivas. I figured he must be a real motorcycle nut, only one in a million in the US would know that Triumph was a motorcycle. So I ask him if he liked Triumphs. His face lit up like a Christmas tree as he explained he loved British motorcycle marques, not just Triumph, but Norton, Vincent, AJS, Matchless. For nearly an hour he rolled out technical information about valves and pistons that simply lost me – ending with an abrupt goodnight and he was gone.

So each night for about a week we'd meet in the bar, chat about the decline of the British motorcycle industry and the rise of the Japanese. I don't remember giving my name or getting his.

One night he asked me if I wanted to go for a ride up into the Hollywood Hills. In the hotel garage he had a Norton. I climbed on behind him and we set off. We ended up on Mulholland Drive, which runs along the top of the mountains dividing Los Angeles from the San Fernando Valley. The engine growled as he opened the throttle and we increased speed alarmingly, swinging into snaky bends faster than I thought possible. I knew it's considered a bit pansy for a pillion rider to grasp the driver but I was forced to as we hurtled through the night angling into chicanes and s-bends. Finally, we turned onto Beverly Glen and headed down to the hotel. I'd barely got off the bike when he took off at speed, running through the gears in a great throaty roar up Wilshire Boulevard.

We met a few more times after that, then one afternoon I was at the hotel pool doing some drawings at a parasoled table. The place was empty except for Carlos, a lifeguard. I heard someone say 'hi' and saw my motorcycle buddy hurrying by. I waved, he waved back and then ducked into the hotel. Carlos looked startled. He hurried around the pool and said:

'Do you know who that is?'

I was about to say it was my motorcycling drinking buddy but Carlos was too quick:

'That's Steve McQueen.'

Steve McQueen! My face dropped in shock. At that moment I looked up and across the pool behind a window my hairy friend was watching. He must have seen Carlos rush over to talk to me and got suspicious. I never saw him again, or Carlos, who got fired.

As for the movie, that too got fired – a change in senior executives at Universal passed on the project and I headed back to Norfolk to lick my wounds and elbow a few Adnams.

I was at Jonathan Cape, the publishers, sometime in the summer of 1975, when one of the editors, Valerie Kettley, handed me a poem and asked if I could guess the name of the author.

> Ahoy! The old *Alcestis*,
> The Spaniards' bane and death,
> That sails the thirteenth parallel
> Before the trade winds' breath.

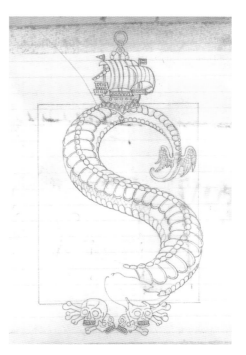

It sounded like John Masefield to me, the Poet Laureate when I was growing up, so that is who I said. She told me it was by Richard Adams, author of the phenomenally successful fantasy novel *Watership Down*. Apparently he wanted me to illustrate the poem. I met Richard and we talked about Tom de Chat, the hero of *The Ship's Cat*. There were to be thirteen plates and illustrated initial letters at the beginning of each page of verse. So once again I was off to the beautiful Reading Room at the British Museum, as well as to the Maritime Museum at Greenwich, doing three months' of research into the design of Elizabethan galleons, ships' rigging, pirate dress and so forth. And many Norfolk cats were coerced into posing for the book.

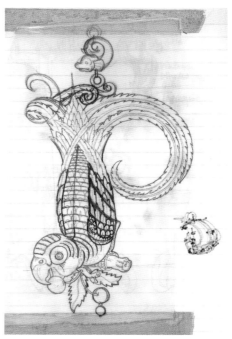

The Ship's Cat by Alan Aldridge and Richard Adams, published by Jonathan Cape, London, 1977.
Right Sketches.
Opposite Front cover.
Overleaf Four of the colour plates and sketch of a galleon as an initial letter G.

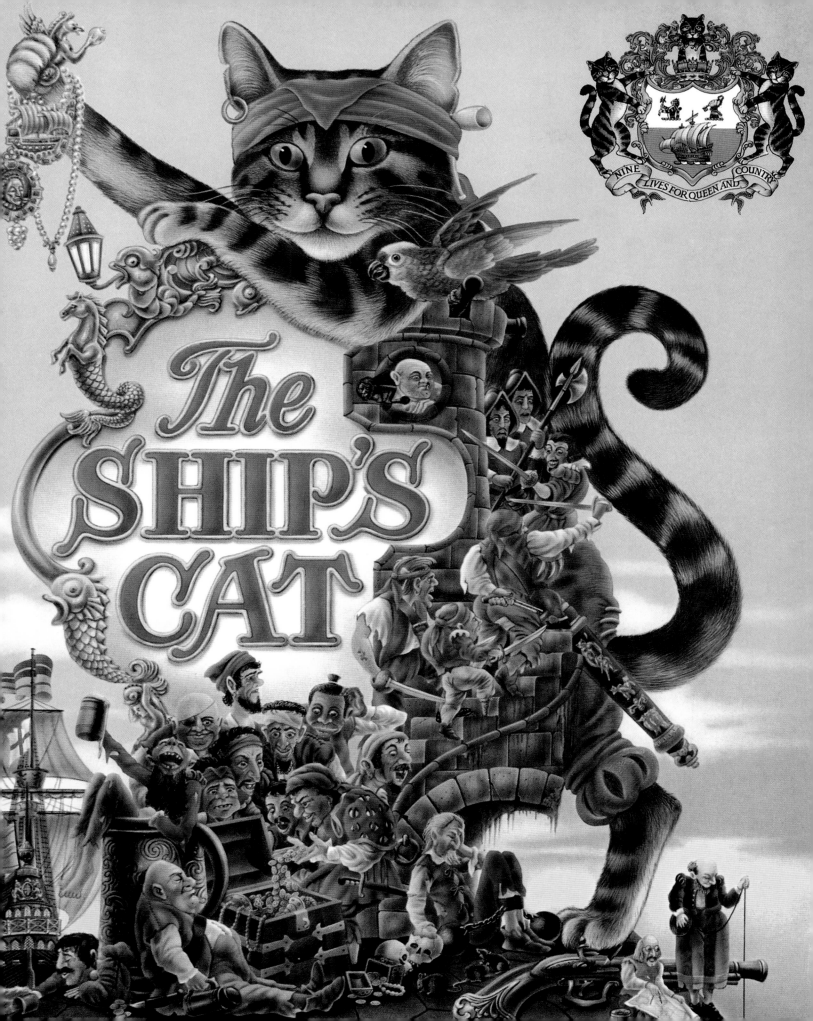

NINE LIVES FOR QUEEN AND COUNTRY

The SHIP'S CAT

Billboard illustrations and sketch
for Heineken campaign, 1977.

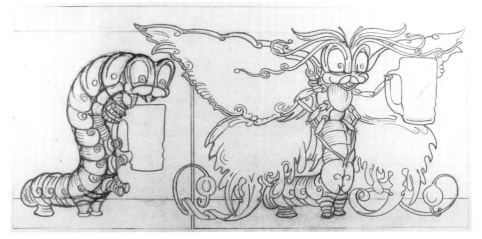

her beers cannot reach.

Heineken refreshes the parts other beers cannot reach.

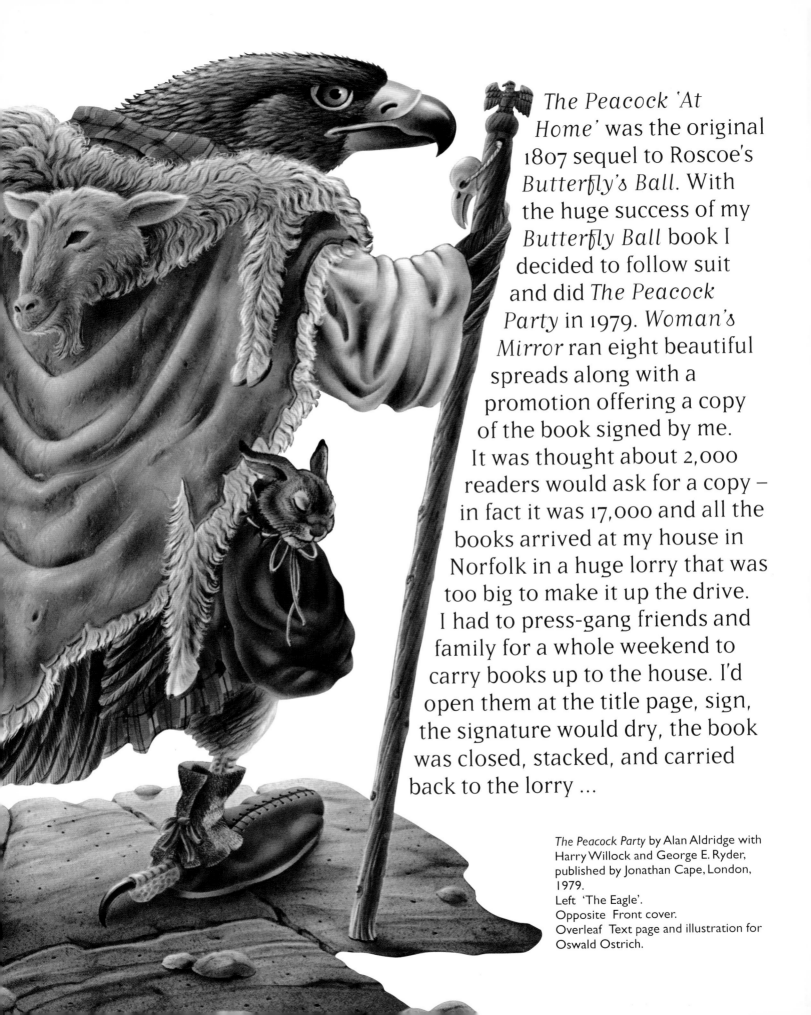

The Peacock 'At Home' was the original 1807 sequel to Roscoe's *Butterfly's Ball*. With the huge success of my *Butterfly Ball* book I decided to follow suit and did *The Peacock Party* in 1979. *Woman's Mirror* ran eight beautiful spreads along with a promotion offering a copy of the book signed by me. It was thought about 2,000 readers would ask for a copy – in fact it was 17,000 and all the books arrived at my house in Norfolk in a huge lorry that was too big to make it up the drive. I had to press-gang friends and family for a whole weekend to carry books up to the house. I'd open them at the title page, sign, the signature would dry, the book was closed, stacked, and carried back to the lorry ...

The Peacock Party by Alan Aldridge with Harry Willock and George E. Ryder, published by Jonathan Cape, London, 1979.
Left 'The Eagle'.
Opposite Front cover.
Overleaf Text page and illustration for Oswald Ostrich.

The Peacock Party

AN INVITATION FROM
ALAN ALDRIDGE
WITH
HARRY WILLOCK
AND
GEORGE E. RYDER

A SEQUEL TO
THE BUTTERFLY BALL

OSWALD OSTRICH, R.A.

Cranes came from Egypt and larks from Brazil;
The Ostrich loped down from his house on the hill.

Oswald Ostrich, R.A.
Has, on any given day:
Bats in the Belfry
Lions in the Den
Locusts in the Oven
Gravy on his Pen
Gold coins in woolly socks
Turtles in the Pool
Cheetahs in the Card-Room
Whales in the Hall
Lilies in the Tea Pot
Banknotes in the Shed
Honey on the Chandelier
Snakes asleep in bed
Beggars in the Bathroom
Watches baked in batter
Monkeys in the Studio
— As mad as a hatter.

'The Peacock Party'.

'Madame Bella Donna'.

Opposite, clockwise from top left 'Sir Perceval Peacock Proposes a Party', 'Dodo's Dream', 'The Tailor Bird', 'The Raven'.

128

I was asked to decorate the Shadow racing team's car for the 1979 Formula One season. The driver Jan Lammers, in his debut season for F1, was from Holland and the team was sponsored that year by the Dutch tobacco company Samson. I used the company's lion logo as a starting point for the design. No Grand Prix car ever looked like this and it created a sensation – and later won awards at various Concours d'Elegance around the USA.

Above Jan Lammers driving the DN9B. **It was not a very competitive car and Shadow's best result was fourth place, achieved by Lammers's team-mate, Elio de Angelis, at the US Grand Prix, 7 October 1979.**

The LION'S CAVALCADE

BY ALAN ALDRIDGE

WITH
HARRY WILLOCK
POEMS BY
TED WALKER

Following *The Butterfly Ball* and *The Peacock Party*, I decided to do a third book in order to sell all three as a boxed set. That never happened although Jonathan Cape published the book in 1980. Unlike the other two volumes, *Lion's Cavalcade* had no precedents. The illustrations were based on exotic animals and once all the pictures were completed I asked the poet and dramatist Ted Walker to write the poems.

I'd spent seven years illustrating *Butterfly Ball, Ship's Cat, Peacock Party* and *Lion's Cavalcade* and I was all picture-booked out. I'd enjoyed my stint developing *Captain Fantastic* in the US and my local pub in Norfolk was losing its charm. The siren lure of Hollywood invaded my dreams.

The Lion's Cavalcade by Alan Aldridge with Harry Willock and Ted Walker, published by Jonathan Cape, London, 1980.
Opposite Front cover.
Right 'The Gorilla Circus'.
Overleaf left 'The Jaguar Lady'.
Overleaf right 'The Company of Porke'.

Opposite 'The Fakir.'
Below left 'Calculus, Lord Chamberlain'.
Below right 'Lord of the Jungle'.
Overleaf left 'The Epic Procession' (detail).
Overleaf right 'Wu Cheng-En' (detail).

Pandemonium was to be a tiny book, about the size of those by Beatrix Potter. I worked on it on and off over a number of years. It started out as *An ABC of Fascinating Flights of Faery Fantasy, a Book of Alliterations* but I ran out of alliterations – what do you do for k, z, x, u – so the book morphed into *Pandemonium: An Alphabet of the Secret Kingdom of Elves, Gnomes and Goblins.* The project got shelved so that I could do Captain Fantastic. Shown here are P for Punch, Poppies, Pan, Puss-in-Boots; I for Imps; E for Elves and Eagle; and the rough for the *Pandemonium* front cover.

Phantasia began as an adventure story about a young boy, Billy Grimpil, being abducted into fairyland. However, it looked as if it was going to take about five years to complete so I decided to add the finished drawings to an illustrated autobiography. This included a selection of my work to date and I put it together in 1980. It was shortly after this that I decided to move to Los Angeles. Maybe, just maybe, I could start a whole new career there – switch from being the 'Aubrey Beardsley in Blue Jeans' of the seventies to movie mogul in the eighties. I packed my toothbrush and headed west ...

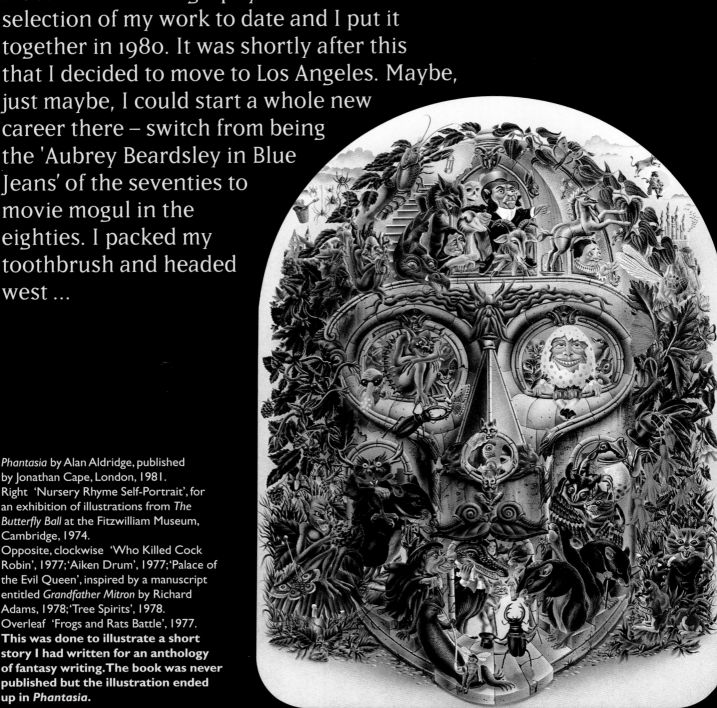

Phantasia by Alan Aldridge, published by Jonathan Cape, London, 1981.
Right 'Nursery Rhyme Self-Portrait', for an exhibition of illustrations from *The Butterfly Ball* at the Fitzwilliam Museum, Cambridge, 1974.
Opposite, clockwise 'Who Killed Cock Robin', 1977; 'Aiken Drum', 1977; 'Palace of the Evil Queen', inspired by a manuscript entitled *Grandfather Mitron* by Richard Adams, 1978; 'Tree Spirits', 1978.
Overleaf 'Frogs and Rats Battle', 1977. **This was done to illustrate a short story I had written for an anthology of fantasy writing. The book was never published but the illustration ended up in *Phantasia*.**

COL. PARKER

'The music business is a cruel and shallow money trench, a long plastic hallway where thieves and pimps run free and good men die like dogs, for no good reason. There's also a negative side.'

Hunter S. Thompson

'Colonel' Tom Parker was Elvis Presley's legendary manager and by all accounts a right royal rascal. It was rumoured that towards the end of Elvis's career the jolly ol' Colonel took fifty per cent of the King's earnings, then skimmed all his own expenses straight off the top of Elvis's remaining fifty per cent. This still left Elvis with plenty of money to throw around on fried peanut butter and banana sandwiches and one-night stands with adolsecent groupies and *Playboy* bimbos.

I had an interesting adventure with the Colonel. I was in Hollywood in 1981, looking for some kind of yellow brick road into the movie business. Things were slow. I'd wandered from one film studio meeting to another trying to sell a couple of projects I'd written: a modern-day version of Bluebeard and Toytown Murders, a crime thriller involving the mysterious death of Humpty Dumpty, bludgeoned to an egg salad by a pair of smoked haddocks! I was getting the proverbial run-around by studio executives with one eye on the clock, anxious to get back to their casting couch.

I needed a quick earner, something in publishing that would keep me occupied for about a year, until I got my scripts funded. I had the idea to do a book, the *Elvis Illustrated Lyrics*, along the lines of the *Beatles Illustrated Lyrics*. I put together a presentation: a few illustrations for songs such as 'Heartbreak Hotel' and 'Hound Dog'. Now I had to find the Colonel.

I learnt that the Colonel held court with his good old boys (mistakenly referred to in the press as 'The Memphis Mafia' – those were a bunch of friends and yes men who lived and worked with Elvis), in a suite somewhere in the RCA building on Sunset. Getting a show-biz

legend on the phone was another matter. After a couple of weeks of getting the same old routine from the RCA telephonist – 'Sorry, Colonel Parker doesn't have offices here' and the line going dead – I was ready to give up on the Elvis book.

Talk about Kismet and the planets being propitiously aligned: at a party I was introduced to a guy who claimed to be a business associate of the Colonel's. Before he could slide off into the crowd I moved in and quickly dropped the Beatles name a few times and said I had a project to pitch to the Colonel. He smiled an array of dazzlingly white teeth the size of tombstones and explained that the Colonel rarely gave meetings and when he did you got a minute, maybe two, to do your spiel before being politely ejected. I smiled like a wolf at meat and said, 'A minute would be more than adequate.'

We laughed and swapped phone numbers. I didn't expect to hear from Mr Tombstoneteeth. I did.

Two days later he called. The Colonel would meet me at his eighth-floor suite in the RCA building on Friday at five o'clock. 'Don't be late! The Colonel is a stickler for punctuality. He's off to Vegas for the weekend – he's gonna give you a whole minute and thirty seconds.'

Friday: the sun was microwaving the city. I got a cab. I assumed the driver would know where the RCA building was. He didn't and the traffic on Sunset sucked. I was gonna be late. At RCA, the receptionist, a pretty punkette, gasped when I entered late and sweaty. She stared at me bug-eyed and agitated. I told her I had a meeting with Colonel Parker. She got the shakes and slowly raised her finger and pointed at me. For a moment I thought she was going to acuse me of 'flashing' her but she stammered, 'Joe'.

Joe I wasn't and I was late for the Colonel.

'Joe?'

'You're Joe Strummer!' She squealed and rolled her eyes.

Who was Joe Strummer? (I learned later he was lead singer of the Clash.) Who cared? I was late for the 'Man' and some ditzy groupie was messing me about. The lobby clock was at 5.10.

'My name ain't Joe, it's Alan, Alan Aldridge.'

The punkette was not listening; she thrust a pencil and notepad at me.

'Can I get your autograph please, Joe?' She was hyperventilating.

The elevator door opened. It was 5.15. Damn Joe, damn signing bits of paper. I jumped into the elevator, scanned the buttons and punched eight and hoped it was the right floor. It was. The elevator door opened onto a fancy reception with pictures of Elvis and gold records plastered on the walls. A secretary gave me the evil eye as I staggered out of the elevator.

'Alan Aldridge,' I said.

'You're late,' she snarled. She picked up the telephone.

'Mr Aldridge is here,' said with the malevolent boredom of a razor blade. She listened briefly then put the phone down. She stood up and pushed a large door ajar. A thick rope of cigar smoke snaked out into the reception area and with it lots of good ol' boy cackle.

'The Colonel is anxious to get off to Vegas. Be advised to be quick.'

I stepped into the room. It was a twilight zone, just a couple of dim sconces glowed dully through heavy smoke. A board table ran the length of the room, littered with bottles, cans, and ash trays piled with dog-ends. There must have been ten old guys sitting around the table, drinking whiskey, joking around. It was as if I was invisible, nobody looked at me – maybe they couldn't see me for smoke.

'Well, well, it's the Englishman.' The room immediately went quiet. Heads turned my way. Must be the Colonel. Now I could see him, fat and jolly at the head of the table, smoking a huge cigar, like a Zeppelin crashed into his mouth.

'Boys, this is Mr Aldridge, he's a friend of the Beatles and has flown all the way from London especially to see us.'

Whoa. I'd cabbed it from Hollywood, about two miles max, but if he thought I'd flown 7,000 miles and that enabled me to get a few extra minutes, I was not going to shatter the illusion.

I was given a seat next to the Colonel. I hadn't even sat down before he started rolling out Elvisisms in a well-oiled performance. The man was in his element, chewing the fat and a cigar, reciting poems by the King. Within minutes, he and I got to trading jokes and telling outrageous stories. The rest of the room disappeared. It was just me and jolly ol' Tom shooting the breeze. He re-read me poems Elvis had written,

showed me Elvis 'merch' and pulled out wads of photos of the King. After close on two hours Colonel Tom suddenly realized a) it was seven o'clock and b) we hadn't discussed why I'd come all the way from London (!) to a meeting with him.

'So, what you selling, son?'

Gee, I was having such a good time I'd forgotten too. I go into my *Beatles Illustrated Lyrics* sales mode. At the mention of the Beatles the Colonel pulled a face.

'Elvis wasn't crazy about the Beatles.'

Jesus, I thought everyone loved the Beatles. I changed tack and rolled out a bunch of potential sales figures and the millions of dollars that the Elvis book could make. Now I definitely had the Colonel's attention. I pulled out my *Elvis Illustrated Lyrics* book presentation, spread it out on the table, showed the Colonel a mock-up of the front cover and a drawing of 'Heartbreak Hotel'. He loved the concept and gave it the go-ahead. All he wanted was a $50,000 advance immediately. I told him that wouldn't be a problem. We shook hands on the deal and the Colonel gave me six bottles of Elvis white table wine and I left. Mission accomplished.

When I got back to my house the phone was ringing. It was Mr Tombstoneteeth, the guy who'd set up my meeting with the Colonel.

'Hey, Alan, what did you do to the Colonel?' he yelled.

'Do?' I queried.

'You were with him over an hour.'

'Two and a half,' I corrected.

'Hey, kid, even President Nixon didn't get that kinda time. The Colonel thinks you're fantastic, the most charismatic guy he's met since Elvis. He wants to represent you.'

'Represent? What?'

'The Colonel wants to manage you.'

'Manage?'

'Let's meet.'

We met a week later at his home in Calabasas.

'The Colonel wants you to be like a creative consultant for all aspects of Elvis licensing, everything from films to merchandising and publishing. He's offering you a three-year contract.' He shoved a document in front of me.

'You'd get a quarter million dollars the first year, 350 through the next and half a million the third year, with bonuses based on earnings.'

I flicked through the contract not quite believing what I was hearing. But there it all was on page three under 'Compensation'. I met the Colonel again, this time he was alone in his office. He asked me if I was going to sign the contract. I told him I was thinking about it. I asked what he had in mind in terms of work. He explained that to begin with I should go to Memphis and report back on ways to develop the Elvis brand. Secondly, he was thinking of putting up a statue of Elvis, something huge and monumental, maybe in solid gold(!), outside the International Hotel Las Vegas, where Elvis made his famous comeback in 1969 and played regularly until his death in 1977. The Colonel smiled, 'Start on it right away.'

I flew to Memphis, did the tour of Graceland, then went across the street to where a tatty mall sold Elvis memorabilia. The next time I met the Colonel was at his apartment on Wilshire. We discussed what I'd seen in Memphis, then talked about the statue, how it had to be heroic, like the Marine Corps war memorial of the raising of the flag on Iwo Jima. Contrary to his traditional approach, I was thinking something more rock'n'roll, an inflatable, say around 150 feet.

I kept this to myself and started to put together some sketches. The idea was to have a huge gold box, say 30-feet high, inscribed with Elvis's discography, biography and filmography. Every four hours the top would open and a huge inflatable Elvis would slowly uncurl, rising to a massive 150–70 feet. A light show would be projected on the skin of the statue. After ten minutes Elvis would slowly deflate back into the box.

At the same time, I was talking to publishers about the *Elvis Illustrated Lyrics* and had a lot of interest. I was looking to get the $50,000 advance for the Colonel, when I found a worm in the apple. The Colonel didn't own the rights to the lyrics of the major songs recorded by Presley: 'Heartbreak Hotel', 'Jailhouse Rock', 'Blue Suede Shoes', 'Don't Be Cruel'. To have to deal with all kinds of rights' owners would be a nightmare. I went cold turkey on the book idea. Seems the old Colonel was trying to pick up a fast $50,000 he wasn't entitled to!

I got a call from the Colonel asking me over to RCA right away. He wanted an immediate Elvis idea for the lobby of the International Hotel (which was now the Las Vegas Hilton), something exclusive, something he could own that would make him ready cash, daily. He gave me a long list of what it couldn't be: mugs, plates, T-shirts, plastic dolls. He'd already sold those licences. I'd heard that the Colonel had big gambling debts and I figured he wanted to earn some quick readies.

'How's the contract, ready to sign?', he asked.

'Yeah, just waiting to hear back from my lawyer,' I replied. I didn't have a lawyer. I didn't have the heart to to tell him I was losing interest in the deal.

For the lobby, I came up with the 'Throne of the Rock'n'Roll King'. It would be a multi-media dais where people could sit and have a Polaroid picture taken of themselves surrounded by Elvisania, including screens with footage of the King's films and television shows. The Colonel loved

the sideshow look of it. He immediately figured a $15 price tag per photograph – at the rate of one every minute, that would be about $13,500 a day and $4,927,500 a year. No wonder he called me a genius.

I needed help with the Colonel's contract. To sign or not to sign, that was the question. I called my agent, Bobby Littman, for advice. A couple of nights later I was at Bobby's house, sharing a Jacuzzi with him. It was a full moon and he was smoking a huge joint and downing vodka Martinis. I made do with a bottle of Krug. He'd spent the past half hour trawling through the Colonel's contract and didn't look happy.

'Well, Aldridge.' Bobby always called me Aldridge – he played being very English and spoke with regal pompousness. 'Do you want to be in the Elvis business or in the movie business?'

Simple question but not such a simple answer. Basically I wanted to be in the money-making business.

'What d'you mean Robert?'

Bobby sucked heavily on his joint, grinning evilly, 'Simple, dear boy, are you in Hollywood to make movies or do you want to design porcelain teacups that promote an overweight, dead pop singer?'

'Don't be cruel Bobby. We're talking about the King. But put like that I guess I want to be in movies.'

'Look, don't worry about money, if you need $250,000 I can get you that, easy, just give me a movie idea to sell. Let me tell you, Aldridge, if you think getting your money out of the Colonel is going to be easy, think again. One fuck up on your part, old son, and you'll be pushing up cactii in the desert.'

Like all things that sound too good to be true, my deal with the Colonel quickly fell apart. Designing stuff for Elvis didn't have the allure and glamour of movies, and I was already writing my next big adventure, called the Mother Goose Mystery.

I never signed the contract and Bobby never did get me the $250,000 …

International Hotel, Las Vegas, 1982. Left Concept sketch for the 'Throne of the Rock'n'Roll King' in the lobby. Opposite Concept sketch for inflatable statue of Elvis Presley.

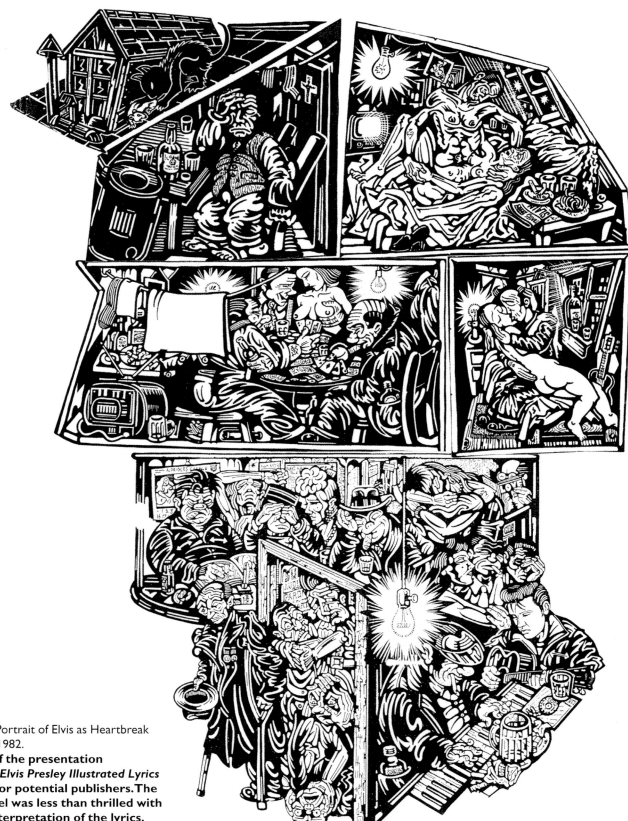

Right Portrait of Elvis as Heartbreak
Hotel, 1982.
**Part of the presentation
of the *Elvis Presley Illustrated Lyrics*
book for potential publishers. The
Colonel was less than thrilled with
this interpretation of the lyrics.**

Opposite *Opium, Heavenly Demon* by
John Veron, book cover, 1999.
**I received an e-mail from a gentleman
in Bangalore claiming to have met me
at Sai Baba's ashram in Puttaparthi
(see pp. 161–66). He wanted me to do
a cover for *Opium*, which his company
was going to publish. 'Sure, I'll do it,' I
said (even though I didn't remember
him). He sent the relevant information
– dimensions, author, etc. – and I got
to work. I shipped the cover and
never heard another word – happens
sometimes. You have to say to
yourself, the journey is what matters.
Nice cover though!**

OPIUM
Heavenly Demon

JOHN VERON

THE GNOLE: PLAYING GOD

To begin at the beginning. What gave me the idea to write the novel *The Gnole*?

Was it the article in *New Scientist* magazine suggesting that there are more creatures on earth than have yet been found and that therefore the Loch Ness monster, Bigfoot, the Yeti and many other large animals could exist, waiting to be discovered.

Or was it Ruth Montgomery's book *The World Before*, which discusses Atlantis and proposes that the Atlanteans barely existed on the physical plane and were more like spirits or ghosts? She describes how the Atlanteans caught small creatures who lived underground and taught them to do tasks of manual labour. According to Montgomery, these creatures were about three feet (one metre) tall, furry, mole-like and bipedal, in the way that raccoons often stand on two feet. To me, they sounded like a cross between gnomes and my favourite creatures, moles: this gave birth to gnoles.

Gnoles would keep me busy for the next eight years. I put together a basic story outline. Gnoles are small of size and wise in wit. They are friendly, furry folks who live in neat and comfy homes deep in the wild woods of the Smoky Mountains in the present-day United States. Gnoles have a love of nature and all living creatures. Sadly, with the destruction of forests, the gnoles have become shy and rare.

Gnolidae Erectus Americanus

The name of our hero is Fungle Foxwit – a mage or shaman of sorts, wise in the arts of alchemy, the healing properties of plants, and in magic spells and lores commanding the elements of earth, air, fire and water. Other characters include Neema, his girlfriend; Ka, a gnome and Fungle's best buddy; Conker, a tree spirit, and Molom, Lord of the Forests. I created quirky foes too: Thorn, the oozlumps and the demon Theverat.

Molom gives Fungle an urgent mission: the ancient stone Baphomet, which destroyed Atlantis, has surfaced in America and Fungle must find and destroy the stone before Theverat finds it and turns the earth into the wasteland predicted by the Mayans.

Fungle's adventures result in his capture by humans who take him to New York, where he becomes a media phenomenon. Likeable, magical, witty and wise he captures the affections of the world until the Department of Parapsychic Research, a secret government unit, sequesters Fungle in its guarded facility and begins conducting experiments on him. Fungle escapes with the help of Ka

The Gnole by Alan Aldridge, written with Steve Boyett and illustrated with Maxine Miller and Harry Willock, published by William Heinemann, 1991.
Above *Gnolidae Erectus Americanus*.
Left Fungle Foxwit and his friend Ka chinwag by the fireside.
Opposite Front cover.

ALAN ALDRIDGE

STEVE BOYETT • MAXINE MILLER

and together they head back to the Smoky Mountains for a final confrontation with Theverat and the destruction of the stone Baphomet.

In conjunction with the basic storyline, I did drawings of the main characters. My next step was to present the story to my agent, Bobby Littman. We talked about which publishers we should offer it to in New York or whether to develop it as a movie. Bobby said he'd get back to me.

The gnole idea quickly became an obsession. In my own mind I was thinking of it as a book – perhaps a new form of novel, where the story however fantastical would be authenticated by photographs and documentation. I couldn't recall anything like it being attempted before, which only fuelled my interest.

I designed a gnole with a benevolent physiognomy – little, crescent-shaped eyes, much like those of the Buddha – and got famed Hollywood prosthetics man Stan Winston to make a life-size mask. I had forest clothes made from materials such as Indian hemp, wild cotton and cat-tail fibres. I then persuaded Billy Barty, America's most famous 'little person' and a well-known film actor, to wear the mask and clothes, and talked the big-shot LA photographer Norman Seiff into a photo session with Fungle the Gnole. The shoot was amazing – on the set Fungle came alive: danced, joked, played up to the camera, laughed, cried and generally blew everyone away. Later, looking at the 35mm shots, I realized that I was falling into the myth of my own making and beginning to believe gnoles really existed.

While waiting to hear from Bobby about which route we would pursue in selling the gnole idea, I refined my presentation kit to twenty 35mm slides. I would project these using a hand-held carousel and accompany them with a running commentary.

Bobby called, he had a 'punter', a Dr Walton, lined up. He was a wealthy gynaecologist with a fancy Beverly Hills address who was interested in the gnole

Above left Conkor, a tree spirit.
Left Thorn, a forest goblin.
Opposite above Molom, Lord of the Forest.
Opposite below Ka (full name Karbolic Earthcreep), a gnome and Fungle's best friend.

concept and in putting up development money – say $50,000 – to begin working on a script. I had to meet Dr Walton at 5.30 p.m. the next day.

I duly arrived at Dr Walton's. The waiting room was packed with pregnant women, Beverly Hills types with fake tits and lips the size of settee cushions. I introduced myself to the receptionist, emphasizing that my appointment with Dr Walton was at 5.30 and it was now 5.27. She told me to take a seat. I asked if the reception area had an electrical outlet I could use. She said she thought so but why didn't I go ahead and look. I found one and plugged in the carousel – switched it on and everything was working okay.

It was 5.45 and there were still five very pregnant ladies waiting to be seen. They discussed dilation numbers and whether they were going for a natural birth or an epidural. I figured I was going to be sitting waiting for the doctor until 7 p.m. Oh well, if he put up $50,000 it would be worth it.

I was way off on the time – he finally appeared at 8.20. And gave me quite a shock. The name Walton reeks of Englishness: the composer William Walton and Izaak Walton, the author of *The Compleat Angler*. I expected a tall, tanned and handsome man, a film-starry looking gent with a broad but fake smile arrayed with perfect white teeth. What I got was something quite different.

Dr Walton was diminutive, not much bigger than Mini-Me in the *Austin Powers* movies. He did not apologise for being late but just told me to get started. I turned off a table lamp, clicked up the first picture on the carousel – a painting of Atlantis – and began my narration: 'According to Plato, Atlantis was located beyond the Pillars of Hercules, that is beyond the Straits of Gibraltar ...'

I was interupted by a loud snore. The doctor was fast asleep.Out cold. I laughed at the ridiculousness of the situation ... welcome to Hollywood. I decided to carry on and spent the next fifteen minutes showing the slides to an audience of one. Me. I finished, turned on the light, picked up my carousel and left.

The following morning I had a call from Bobby.

'Clever boy, Aldridge. The doctor loved it. He's ready to write a cheque.'

I told Bobby that the doctor had fallen asleep just as I started the presentation. The only way he could have watched it was from the astral plane. He was zonked out, zzzzzzzzing to his heart's content. He would never put up a dime!

I was right. The doctor stalled parting with his money time and time again. I was to learn that this happens a lot in Tinseltown; people in boring jobs with lots of money want some of the film industry's glamorous fairy dust to rub off on them so they pretend to be investors (angels) just to say that they are in the movie bizz.

Over the next few months I met a veritable A-list of Hollywood's movers and shakers – there was lots of interest but no cigar. Then in about 1983 Bobby called about another meeting, this time with Zoetrope, Francis Ford Coppola's studio. I had to show Lucy Fisher (head of production) my presentation. The day after the encounter Bobby called:

'Pack your toothbrush, old boy, you are off to see the wizard.'

I began to think Bobby had been smoking some herbs.

'Wizard? What are you on about?'

'Coppola, dear boy, he wants to see you in New York, a.s.a.p!'

Coppola was shooting the *Cotton Club* in Manhattan. With the help of a first-class plane ticket and a room at the Waldorf Hotel, courtesy of Zoetrope, I went to New York. I had a breakfast meeting arranged with Coppola at his penthouse suite in the Helmsley Palace Hotel the next day at nine o'clock.

I was up early and on the street by 7.30 a.m. I walked past St Patrick's cathedral. It was open for business. I went in. I lit a few candles for luck and told God that if he blessed me with a film deal and it made a load of money I'd donate most of it to the poor!

I reached the Helmsley Palace at 8.57. Perfect. The lobby looked like a Disneyland Versailles. I went to reception, dropped Coppola's name and was ushered into a private elevator, where a uniformed flunky whisked me to the penthouse.

Top Theverat, a demon.
Bottom Baphomet, an evil spirit.

The elevator door opened onto a gorgeous suite. The first thing I noticed was a silver tray with a magnificent spread of coffee, juice and comestibles worthy of the Sun King himself. Great, I thought. I was hungry.

I was greeted by a pretty young woman. I didn't understand what she mumbled in a vague European accent, something about a butler or was it butter will serve or serviette breakfast? I asked for an electical outlet and plugged in the carousel. And then I waited ... and waited ... and waited. Where was the butler?

And where was Coppola? I was sweating and beginning to lose my nerve. The girl kept smiling and my stomach started rumbling.

A man entered. He was wearing a hotel bathrobe of white towelling and was dripping wet. Jesus, I thought, is this the butler? He didn't say a word, just flopped into a chair and nodded. The girl told me in her mumbly voice that I could start.

START? Where was Coppola and, more importantly, where was the butler?

The 'dripping man' looked at me sternly and gave me a 'get the fuck on with your show, I'm a busy man and you're a peon' look. I fired up the carousel and began my narration, 'According to Plato, Atlantis lay beyond the Pillars of Hercules ...' and for the next half hour I hit my groove and did the best presentation I've ever done. I turned the carousel off and looked at the 'Dripping Man'. Hey, at least he was still awake.

He sat in silence for what seemed an eternity and then said very slowly, struggling to find the words, 'Ala [he dropped the n from my name] ... I ... er ... donut ... unnersand.'

Donut unnersand?

Jesus Christ, I'd flown 3,000 miles to pitch to a guy who couldn't speak English.

The girl mumbled a thank you for coming and steered (not quite a bum's rush) me to the elevator. I wanna protest but don't. Before I could say 'ow's yer father', I was in the elevator

Top Fungle flying in his magnetite-powered Lunabird.
Bottom Fungle climbs through the dense woods towards the summit of the Mound of the Dead.

and out onto Madison, avenue of broken dreams. I thought of returning to St Patrick's and stealing my candle money from the coin box.

I got back to the Waldorf half expecting to have to pay for my room, but it had been taken care of. I took a cab to the airport and flew back to LA. Screw movies, I'd had enough of imbecilic film meetings.

In the end, *The Gnole* would be a novel, published by William Heinemann in September 1991.

Opposite above Theverat, in his meeting with Fungle, materializes as a silver teapot.
Opposite below Drawing of Fungle entering Tobacco Inn.
Right Fungle makes the front cover of *Rolling Stone*, part of the fictional authentication of the story.
Below *Fungle's Adventures Out and About in Modern America.* A comic strip for an unpublished junior edition (for children aged ten and under) of *The Gnole*, 1993.

HOUSE OF BLUES

I first met Isaac Tigrett in early 1970 outside the Great American Disaster (GAD) restaurant on London's Fulham Road.

I'd done the logo and a poster for GAD, commissioned by its owner Peter Morton (see p. 92). GAD had caused a sensation in London simply by serving a decent hamburger, American style: quarter- or half-pound burgers being the norm, in contrast to the British Wimpy burger, which at the time was exactly as its name implied, a wimpy one-eighth-inch thick piece of greasy meat slapped between a dried bun.

Peter called me, said he had someone I should meet. I went over to the restaurant that evening and he took me outside to where a two-tone (black and robin's egg blue) Bentley R-Type was parked. The retractable roof was open and some hard, southern rock, say Lynnard Skynnard, was blasting out along with thick plumes of highly fragrant smoke.

I pulled open the door and climbed in the back. Sitting there like some pasha was Isaac, a vaguely Jesus-looking guy, bearded and with long hair, and between the thick columns of smoke and shadows I saw his eyes – they were heart-stoppingly blue, like bottled sky, piercing, wired to some cosmic energy available to only a few special people. The eyes locked on to me, he greeted me in a southern States accent and we shook hands. Thirty-eight years later we're still the best of friends.

Later that year, Peter and Isaac joined forces on a restaurant concept called Hard Rock Cafe. Isaac got me to do the logo (see p. 93). Within a few years it became one of the most famous logos in the world. The first Hard Rock Cafe opened near Hyde Park Corner in June 1971 and Isaac put up a poster-size photo of a guy who vaguely looked like Bob Hope with a Jimi Hendrix hairdo – it was Sri Sathya Sai Baba, an Indian guru, and Isaac was a devotee. Isaac took one of Sai Baba's sayings – Love All, Serve All – as an underlying principle for the operation of all Hard Rock Cafes. In 1988, Isaac sold his half of Hard Rock to the British company Pleasurama and reportedly pocketed around $30 million.

Some time later, in 1994, Isaac called me with an idea for a new project: Spirit Channel, an internet one-stop cyber city for those seeking physical and spiritual tranquillity. One year on, despite months of work, Spirit Channel

ground to a halt and died, like a lot of early e-commerce companies.

Then Isaac called, wanting to meet. We got together at his house overlooking LA on Mulholland Drive; he was in a state of messianic fervour, which meant only one thing – a new project! House of Blues was it: a music venue – part voodoo vibe, part blues jook joint. He needed a logo, something that would reflect the deep pain and passion of the blues. So I went into hibernation to do research. I knew nothing about the blues or what a jook joint was. After a month I'd clued into the vibe and got my mojo working, if you know what I mean. Isaac and I met again. We decided the logo should be the Sacred Heart of Jesus; I think we both knew (but didn't say) that it might cause a bit of controversy.

The logo got done and a real estate lot was purchased on Sunset Boulevard. Over a period of eight months, the House of Blues flagship venue took shape. It was a hit from day one. About that time, Isaac and I met at the House of Blues corporate offices on Sunset, right across the street from the new venue. He hit me with a whammy. He wanted me to be the creative director of the House of Blues, full time. I laughed nervously. I hadn't had what my mum

Opposite Initial design for the House of Blues logo, 1995.

Above right Invitation to the opening of the House of Blues in Chicago, 1997. **The interior of the Chicago venue was designed to be like an opera house. The line drawing shows an opera box.**

Below Signage for the House of Blues venue at the Olympic Games, Atlanta, 1996.

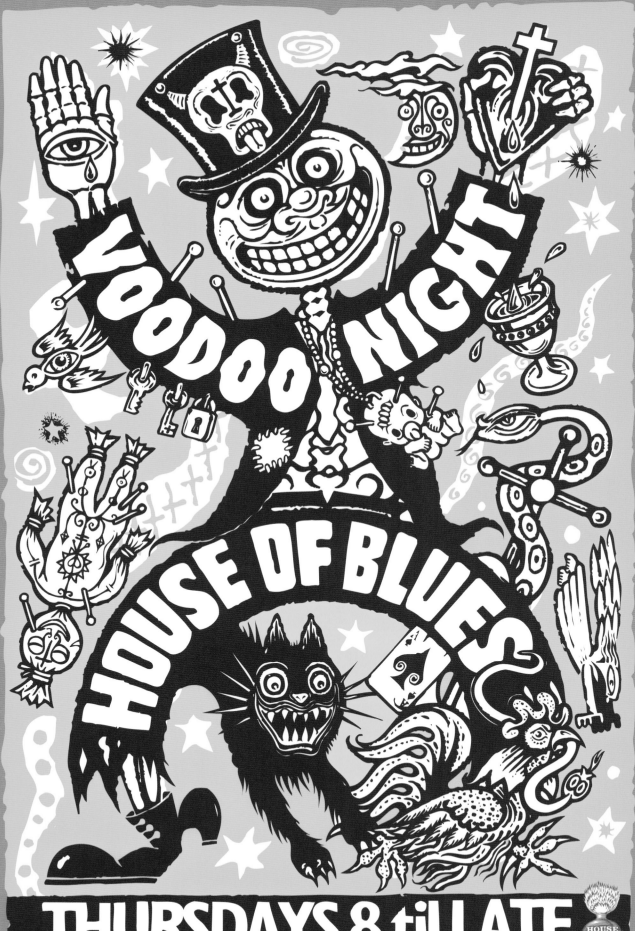

VOODOO NIGHT

HOUSE OF BLUES

THURSDAYS 8 til LATE
INFO/BOXOFFICE1800BLUES4U

HOUSE OF BLUES

would call a real job, a nine-to-five job, since I'd quit Penguin in 1967.

Isaac said money was not a problem and I'd get a bunch of stock options in the company. But there was a proviso: I must travel with him to south India, to Sai Baba's ashram, known as Prasanthi Nilayam (abode of supreme peace), in Puttaparthi, a small town about 75 miles north of Bangalore, and obtain the guru's blessing that I was the right man for the job. As an aside, Isaac informed me that it took him seventeen years to meet Sai Baba, as the guru picks only three people a day for a one-to-one meeting from thousands of devotees, so my chances of getting a personal blessing were remote (probably nonexistent would be more honest) in the five days we would be there.

Despite the high odds, I went. A 20,000 mile round trip for a job I wasn't sure I wanted to meet a holy man I stood no chance of meeting.

Isaac and I flew from Los Angeles via London to Bombay (Mumbai), where we stayed at the Taj President. Then on down to Bangalore, where we arrived at two in the afternoon. A beaten-up old car and a driver met us at the airport. Isaac explained that we had a five-hour drive north to Puttaparthi and that we had to get there before nightfall (7 p.m.) because after dark bandits were on the road.

Bandits! There had been no mention of bandits back in Los Angeles.

Isaac and I sat in the back of the car and we set off at breakneck speed. I soon learnt that traffic in India meanders all over the road, driving in lanes is optional. Isaac fell asleep and I sucked on a bottle of water as villages flashed by until there was just desert and blanketing clouds of dust stirred up by the passing traffic. The sun set and I began to worry about bandits; Isaac snored on. It was pitch black now and the nervous-looking driver assured me that we would be in Puttaparthi in under an hour. His panicky reassurance did nothing to quell my rising fear of being robbed, maybe murdered, in the middle of nowhere. Right on cue with my paranoia, out of the darkness a bunch of skinny Indians wearing turbans and little else, armed with what appeared to be World War I Lee-Enfield rifles, emerged on the road and forced us to stop.

Fuck! Right now I could have been in LA sipping an ice-cold beer.

Opposite and below Event posters for House of Blues Voodoo Night and Jookin', 1996.

Right Sketch of Mick Jagger for CD cover, *Paint It, Blue*, The Rolling Stones, This Ain't No Tribute series, House of Blues Music, 1997.

JOOKIN'

HOUSE OF BLUES

MONDAYS · 8PM-1PM · 1·800·BLUES·4U
HOUSE of BLUES · SUNSET STRIP

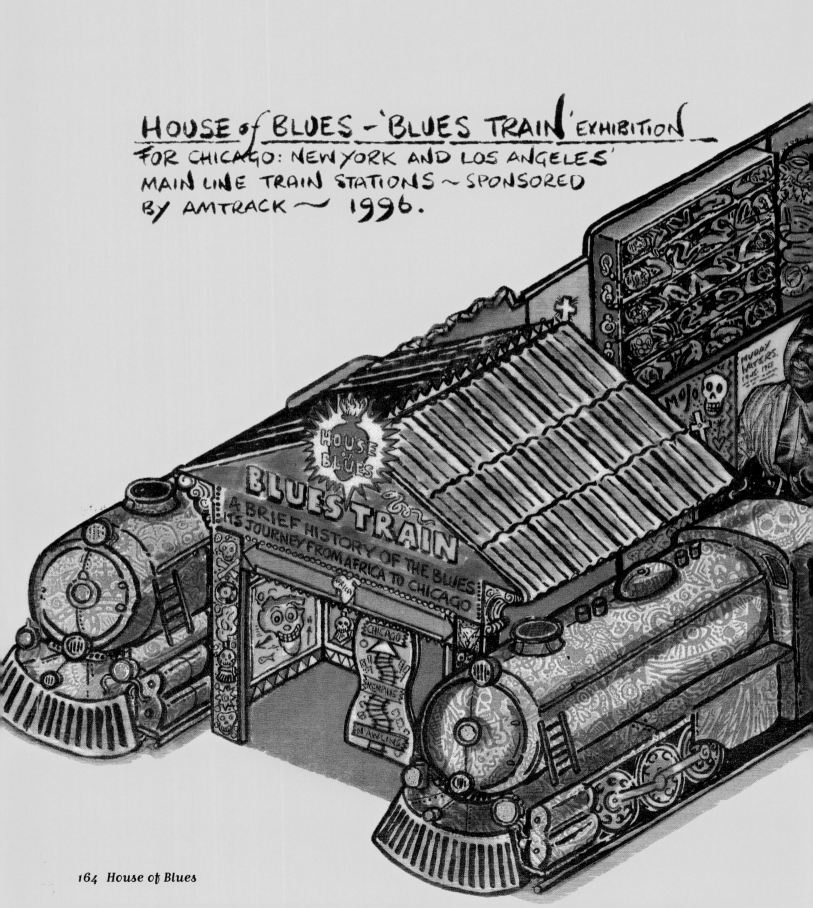

HOUSE of BLUES - 'BLUES TRAIN' EXHIBITION
FOR CHICAGO: NEW YORK AND LOS ANGELES'
MAIN LINE TRAIN STATIONS ~ SPONSORED
BY AMTRACK ~ 1996.

Sketch for House of Blues train exhibition,
in conjunction with Amtrak, 1996.
**This was a touring exhibit showing a
brief history of the blues.**

Below Hog Heaven (not used) and Sin Night posters, 1997.

The bandits pointed their guns aggressively at us, yelling something that I presumed meant we should get out the car. The driver started snivelling and wailing. I elbow-jabbed Isaac awake. He blinked and surfaced back to reality. I quickly explained we are being held up at gunpoint by bandits. Unfussed, he got out of the car and calm as a cucumber walked up to the leader and spoke in a language I did not recognize. The gang stared at me then hurriedly retired into the darkness and Isaac got back into the car.

I asked him what he had said to the bandits. He laughed.

'I told them you were a very special guest of Sai Baba's and that they would all go to Niraya [hell] if any harm befell you.'

I said that as soon as we got to Puttiparthi I wanted to stop at the first bar and get me a large, ice-cold Kingfisher beer in a frosted glass. Isaac hit me with his big, electric-blue eyes and said:

'Al, I didn't want to mention this, 'cos I thought if you knew you might not come to Puttiparthi, but we're in a dry state, there are no bars, no pubs and no alcohol for a thousand miles!'

We arrived at the ashram at eight o'clock. At the front desk we were asked to turn in any pharmaceutical drugs, cigarettes or stimulants of any kind. I reluctantly turned over my Ambien, a sleeping pill I'd been using for some time. We went straight to the dining hall for supper as it was about to close. The food, all vegetarian, was very good. Afterwards we went to Isaac's apartment and unpacked. At nine the lights all over the ashram went out.

Without Ambien I wasn't going to get to sleep. And I didn't until 4.45 a.m. At five, when I was barely into the first level of dreamland, Isaac shook me awake. Time for *darshan*, temple service. I put on my ashram-issue kurta, a knee-length shirt, and hemp slippers and followed Isaac out of the apartment. It was 5.15 a.m. and I expected us to be the only punters going to the temple at such an unearthly hour, but I was dead wrong. Hundreds of people were hurrying along the footpaths – they all seemed to be in a state of happy delirium.

At the entrance to the temple people removed their slippers, threw them on a huge pile and entered the place barefoot through ornate arches.

I followed Isaac inside. The smell of incense was dizzying. There were about five hundred devotees under the roof of the temple, all squatting cheek by jowl, and you could not have squeezed a cigarette paper between them. One side of the temple was open to the elements and outside another thousand followers, maybe more, sat cross-legged. The noise of conversation and singing was like a million wasps. We squatted down and waited.

A film crew from France moved among the crowd.

Suddenly, as if the hand of God had turned off the volume on the remote control, it all went silent. Silence absolute. The Master had arrived. But where? I craned round but couldn't see him. Then across the sea of heads I spotted a saffron gown topped by a Jimi Hendrix hairdo – it was Sai Baba. He drifted through a sea of white kurtas, or rather floated, it was uncanny, as if he was not of this world. I thought of Jesus walking on water.

A feeling of joy overwhelmed me and I didn't know why. I was grinning like an idiot. I was happy – my world of illusion seemed far, far away. Suddenly the crowd gasped. Sai Baba had picked someone for a private interview. Two of his assistants pulled the person from the crowd and escorted him to Sai Baba's private puja (prayer) room. A second person was chosen, one more to go and thousands to choose from. Now I understood why it took seventeen years for Isaac to get picked.

Sai Baba continued his gentle meander through the throng. I was barely paying attention, eyes closed, tripping out on the joy that I was experiencing. The moment was brief, soon someone was grabbing my arms and I was being pulled to my feet ... what the ... the crowd was yelling. I opened my eyes: Sai Baba was in front of me smiling. The film crew whirled around me as I got swept off to the puja room.

An assistant told us, the three chosen ones, to squat, heads bowed, before an ornate chair – you could call it a throne. Sai Baba entered, smelling of tuberose and patchouli, and sat on it. He addressed the man to my right (I was in the middle). His voice was soft and gentle, girlish even, and he delivered a punishing lecture on the ethics of being on time – for business meetings, for family and friends, for everything – ending with the question, 'What does "watch" mean?'

The man replied, 'Only you know, Swami.'

Sai Baba responded, 'Watch means: watch your words, watch your actions, watch your thoughts, watch your character, watch your heart – that is what watch means.'

At this point, Sai Baba stirred the air with his right hand and a gold watch materialized. He gave it to the devotee and said, 'Think of me always. Wear this watch and never be late again.'

Sai Baba now turned his penetrating gaze to me. He held up his hand in front of my face and asked, 'What is this?'

It looked like a hand to me. 'Hand, Swami.'

He giggled. 'Amateur!'

The swami now moved his gaze to the man on my left. Damn, I'd blown it, he'd passed me over, no job and no gold watch. It was a hand. What was I supposed to say. It was a hand, goddamn it. The devotee to the left got the same injunction on being prompt and received a gold watch.

Sai Baba returned to me. He asked (referring with his eyes to the watches), 'Jealous?'

He linked his dark eyes to mine. Holding up his hand, he asked, 'What is this?'

I looked at the hand. I couldn't believe what I was seeing: set in the flat of the palm was an eye. Sai Baba giggled. I was at a loss for words. He got off the 'throne' and told me to follow him. We went into a small room and he closed the door. We faced each other and he spoke in a whisper.

'You worry about your son. You worry he will get into trouble with drugs. He will be fine when he finds his right path and that path is music. You will be proud of him.' How he knew about my son remains a mystery.

Sai Baba stepped closer to me and touched me on the heart. I felt (or did I imagine it?) a surge of energy slam through my body. For a second, I lost my footing but the swami grasped my wrist. Then he moved even closer.

'If you need me, just take one step towards me and I will take a thousand towards you.'

His broad smile told me the meeting was over and I went outside and sat with Isaac. The sun was up, it was a beautiful day.

Later, I was sitting on a lawn reading a book on Sai Baba that I'd bought at a shop in Puttaparthi. Isaac found me and said, 'Hey, Al, the swami tells me you are a very honest, good man and have much creative energy – perfect for House of Blues. You got the job.'

For the next two years my life was taken over with all the madness of a hip company striving to bring a whole new musical experience to the public: designs for T-shirts, TV commercials, books, sauce labels, Mardi Gras flyers, interior designs for new venues, and so on. Everything was done in an adrenalin rush, overnight usually, similar to the experience I'd had at Penguin – and I loved it.

Below Gospel Brunch logo for merchandising and poster, 1996.

Overleaf Vodoo chandelier and elements, developed for the lobby of the House of Blues Hotel, Chicago, 1998 (re-coloured 2005).

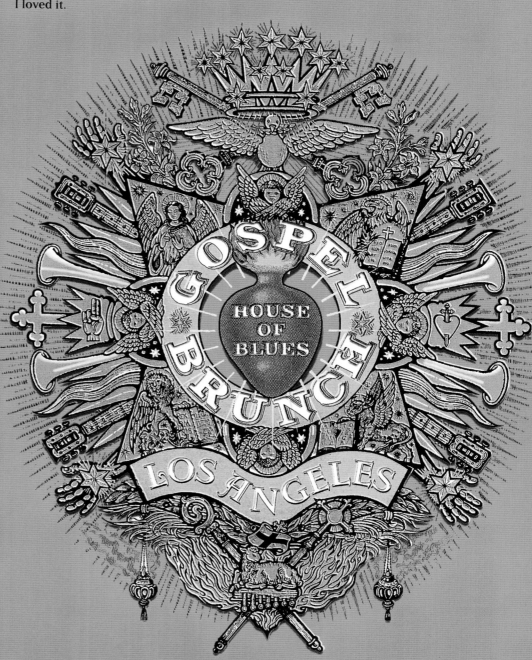

This page and overleaf *Mr Love Pants*, presentation for adult TV series, 1999–2000.

Mr Love Pants, an Ian Drury CD, was released in 1998. I heard the album for the first time in 1999, but it wasn't the music that caught my attention, good as it was, but the name **Mr Love Pants**! I immediately had this vision of a pair of horny men's underpants looking for love in all the wrong places. So I called up Ian and ran my idea past him – his reply was beautiful (like the man), 'Aldridge, mate, you can have anything you want.' I promised I'd get back to him when I had something to show. I'd worked on Mr Love Pants on and off for about six months when I heard of Ian's death in March 2000.

So I decided to put the project on the backburner, where, so far, it has stayed.

LOOKING FOR LOVE IN ALL THE WRONG PLACES!

Tom Ford salutes John Lennon. Illustrations for spreads in *GQ* magazine, September 2001. **Dylan Jones, the editor of the UK edition of GQ magazine, got in touch with me. Tom Ford had a new collection for Gucci celebrating the style of John Lennon and GQ were devoting ten pages to it. Would I do them? Using John's songs as inspiration, I did the illustrations in the form of a ten-page continuous diorama and also art directed the photo shoot.**

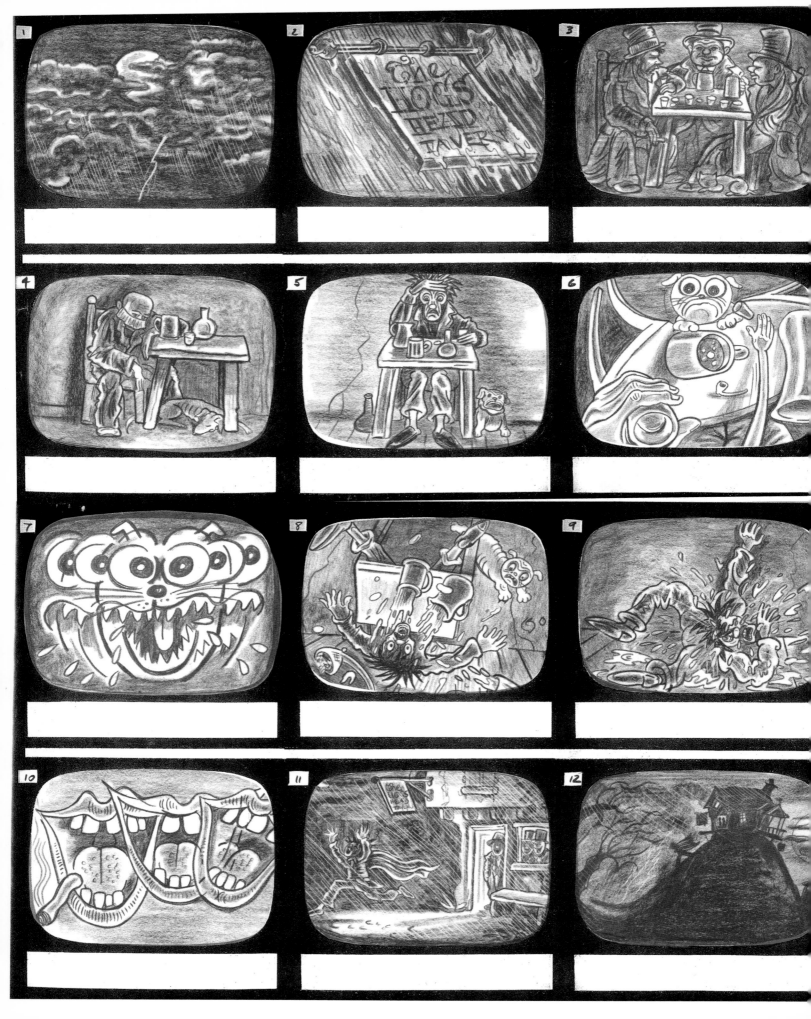

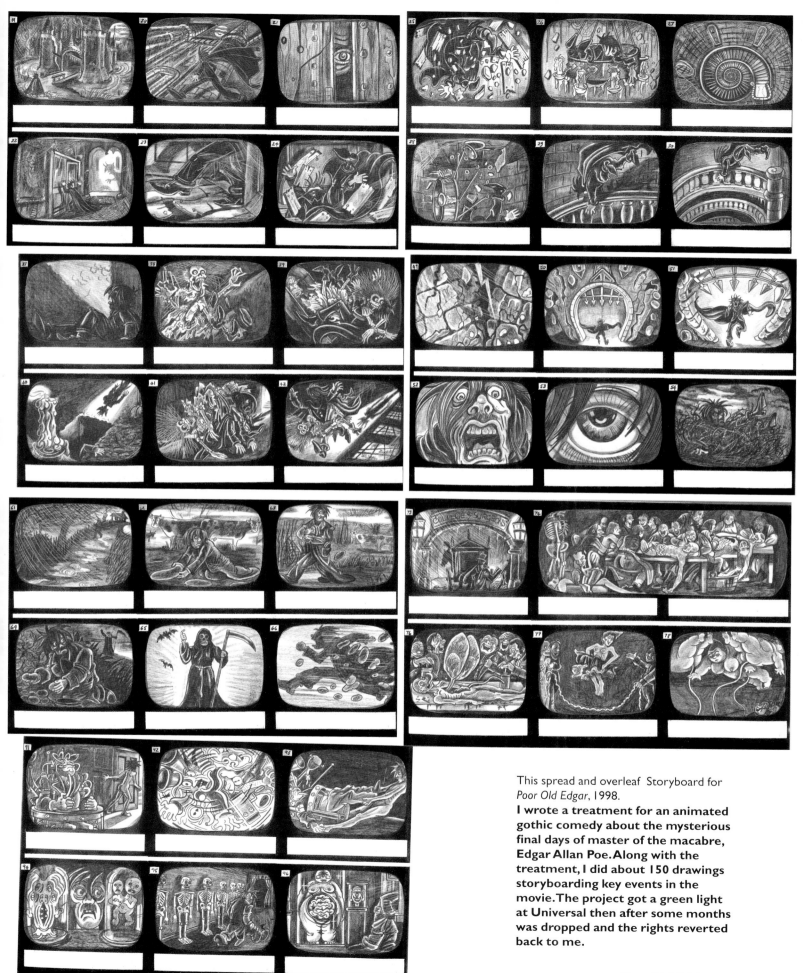

This spread and overleaf Storyboard for
Poor Old Edgar, 1998.
I wrote a treatment for an animated
gothic comedy about the mysterious
final days of master of the macabre,
Edgar Allan Poe. Along with the
treatment, I did about 150 drawings
storyboarding key events in the
movie. The project got a green light
at Universal then after some months
was dropped and the rights reverted
back to me.

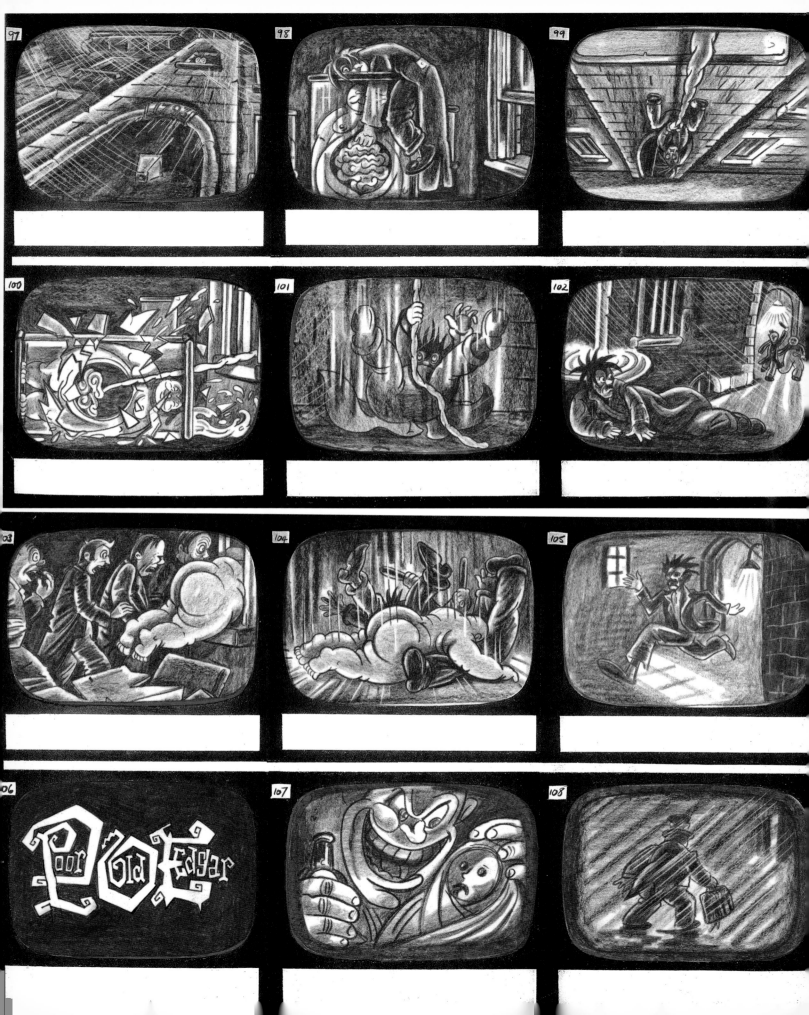

Left CD cover for Benjamin Britten's
War Requiem, 1997.
**Proposed repackaging of a classic
recording for Decca Music.**

Below Cover design for Larry Perick's
unpublished graphic novel, *The Devil &
Mr Tidy*, 1998.
**This was a black comedy about a
retired clerk who falls prey to the
dictates of the Devil.**

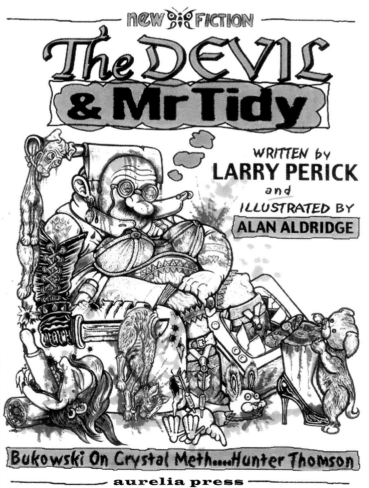

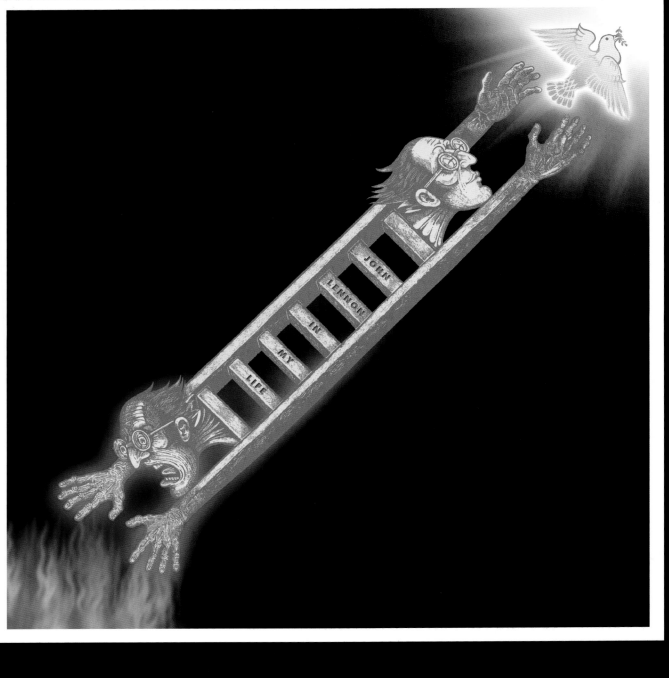

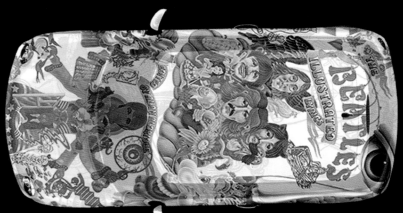

Opposite 'The Greatest Album Covers That Never Were' exhibition, Rock and Roll Hall of Fame, Cleveland, June 2003. **I was one of a hundred artists worldwide who were invited to create a fantasy album cover for their favourite recording star. I chose John Lennon. The album is called** *In My Life.*

Poster and decorated Mini for 'Immaginazione Beatles' exhibition, Rome, October 2002.

1
TITLE CARD
Ornate border. Gold lettering on dark green background.
FADE TO:

2
ext. panoramic view –
english countryside – day.

River lazes through dense woods. In the distance rolling hills shimmer with summer heat. crows and dragonflies swoop and hover above trees.

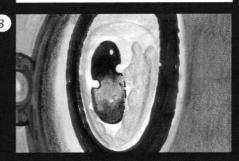

3
extreme closeup – eye
Reflects countryside below.

4
pull back
Reveals face of lord ladybug

5
pull back
Reveals lord and lady ladybug
They hold hands, flying over woods to the Butterfly Ball.

23
int. salty dog tavern – day
closeup – on dandy rat

24
dandy rat with sam stoat.
oswald otter and d'death the fox sit at table and plot nefarious ways to rob the revellers.

25
ext. oakwold tower – day
Victorian folly in state of dilapidation.

26
int. oakwold tower – day
barney bat hangs from roof of tower watching revellers, waiting to prey on an unwary travler!

27
ext. woodland path – day
gnarly gnat dashes through the woods – late for the 'Ball'.

28 INT. BEDROOM – DAY. RUBY HOUSE. A caterpillar, should be on her way to the 'Ball', but dithers, unable to make her mind up whether the skull mask is too scary…or her lipstick too purple!!

35 EXT. BUTTERFLY ARMS – DAY.
PRICKLES THE HEDGEHOG in charge of
'Security' has his hands full ejecting
creatures, particularly NEWTS, the worse
for wear with too much beer!

36 INT. OFFICE – DAY. SIR MONTAGUE
MOUSE wealthy entrepreneur, Financier
of BUTTERFLY BALL sits at his desk
counting the box-office receipts and
worries whether he'll get his money back.

37
EXT. STAGE – DAY
MISS ARANEA SPIDER performs her
remarkable spider-web lassoing act…
FADE TO…

38
MR. CECIL CENTIPEDE plays his special
composition 'Lepidopira Waltz' on his
famous solid gold piano…
CUT TO…

39
FREDDY FROG star of the show, arrives
onstage
aboard 'Peace' float.

40
Fireworks erupt as FREDDY goes into
'Give Peace A Chance'.

53
MONTAGE.
All the DANCERS waltzing, jitterbugging
and jiving!!

midnight,
the BUTTERFLY BALL is over.

54
TITLE CARD

55 EXT. WOODS – NIGHT.
An avenue of FIREFLIES lights the way…
For GUESTS of BUTTERFLY BALL as
they head home to bed. With LORD and
LADY LADYBUG last to leave…

56
Finally, the FIREFLIES wing home.

57
FADE TO BLACK

THE END

Storyboard for proposed animated
children's TV series of *Butterfly Ball* to be
produced by Train Productions, London,
2003. Project not proceeded with.

Left and below Title and characters for *The Toytown Murders*, 1983.

Opposite Title design for *The Mother Goose Mystery*, 2006.

In 1982 I was working in Hollywood as a writer and designer on a half-hour animated special, 'Faeries', produced by Tomorrow's Entertainment for CBS. The show was nominated for four Emmy awards. Tom Moore, president of Tomorrow, asked if I had any other ideas I wanted to develop and I pitched *Toytown Murders*, an animated murder mystery featuring all the popular Mother Goose and nursery-rhyme characters. He bought it and I spent most of 1983 writing the script. In 2006 I resurrected the basic story and redesigned all the characters (overleaf). Now it is *The Mother Goose Mystery*, a feature film, and ready to hit the streets!

MUTANT HONEY PIE   GHOUL VEINROTT   LITTLE LAMB   GEORGY PORGY   SANTA CLAUS KALICO KID   EDDIE

RED.
= For lettering position

The
MOTHER
GOOSE
Mystery ← BLUE

← MAKE IT DARK GREY

DOOR FOR POSITION

SHADOW — EDGES NEED SOFTENING.

OLL   GUMBOOT   JEEVES   JACK FROST   ROCKY ROBOT CROOKED MAN   PUNCHY   OLD WOMAN IN THE SHOE
HUMPTY DUMPTY

The Mother Goose Mystery, 2006. Character sheet showing Three Blind Mice, Humpty Dumpty, the Crooked Man, Simple Simon, the Old Woman Who Lived in a Shoe, Goldilocks, Three Little (Big) Pigs, Insey Winsey Spider and, front centre, the hero of the movie, Eddie Bear, a private detective who sets out to solve the murder of Humpty Dumpty.

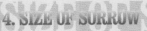

1. EVERYBODY LOVES A HAPPY ENDING

2. CLOSEST THING TO HEAVEN

3. CALL ME MELLOW

4. SIZE OF SORROW

5. WHO KILLED TANGERINE?

6. QUIET ONES

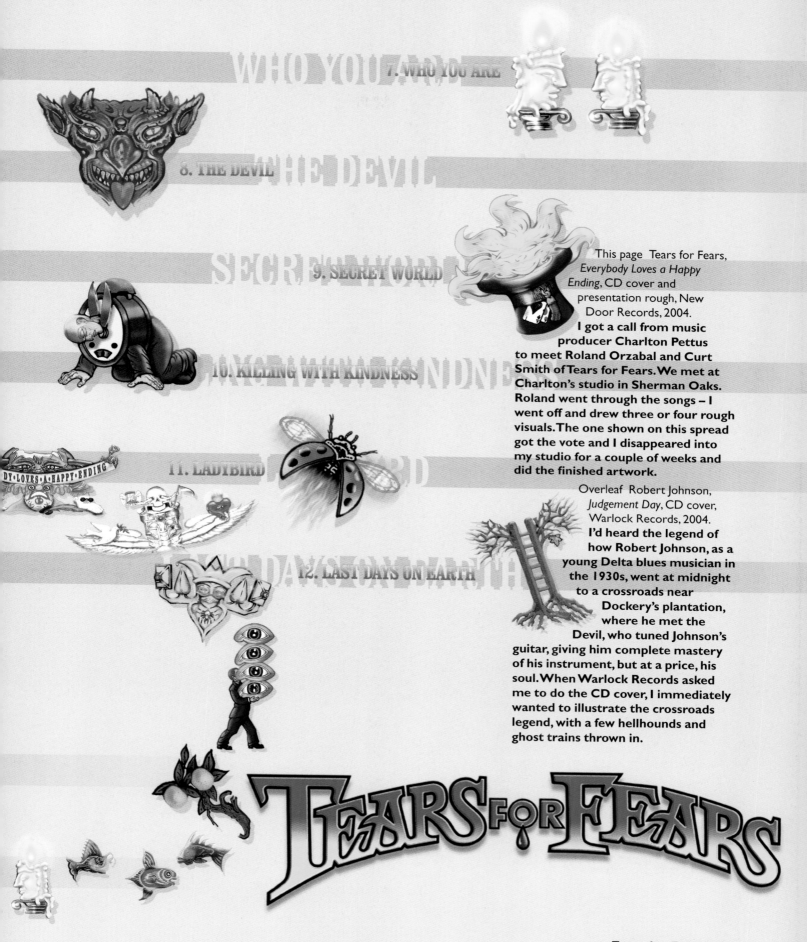

7. WHO YOU ARE

8. THE DEVIL

9. SECRET WORLD

10. KILLING WITH KINDNESS

11. LADYBIRD

12. LAST DAYS ON EARTH

This page Tears for Fears, *Everybody Loves a Happy Ending*, CD cover and presentation rough, New Door Records, 2004.
I got a call from music producer Charlton Pettus to meet Roland Orzabal and Curt Smith of Tears for Fears. We met at Charlton's studio in Sherman Oaks. Roland went through the songs – I went off and drew three or four rough visuals. The one shown on this spread got the vote and I disappeared into my studio for a couple of weeks and did the finished artwork.

Overleaf Robert Johnson, *Judgement Day*, CD cover, Warlock Records, 2004.
I'd heard the legend of how Robert Johnson, as a young Delta blues musician in the 1930s, went at midnight to a crossroads near Dockery's plantation, where he met the Devil, who tuned Johnson's guitar, giving him complete mastery of his instrument, but at a price, his soul. When Warlock Records asked me to do the CD cover, I immediately wanted to illustrate the crossroads legend, with a few hellhounds and ghost trains thrown in.

ROBERT JOHNS

JUDGEMENT D

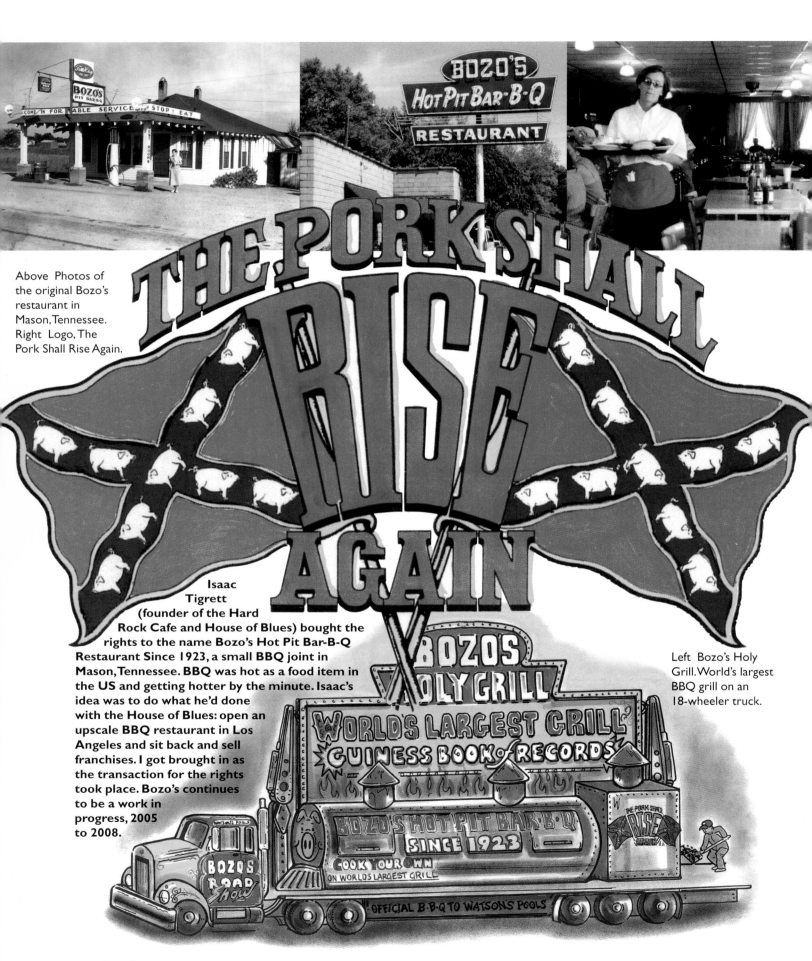

Above Photos of the original Bozo's restaurant in Mason, Tennessee. Right Logo, The Pork Shall Rise Again.

THE PORK SHALL RISE AGAIN

Isaac Tigrett (founder of the Hard Rock Cafe and House of Blues) bought the rights to the name Bozo's Hot Pit Bar-B-Q Restaurant Since 1923, a small BBQ joint in Mason, Tennessee. BBQ was hot as a food item in the US and getting hotter by the minute. Isaac's idea was to do what he'd done with the House of Blues: open an upscale BBQ restaurant in Los Angeles and sit back and sell franchises. I got brought in as the transaction for the rights took place. Bozo's continues to be a work in progress, 2005 to 2008.

Left Bozo's Holy Grill. World's largest BBQ grill on an 18-wheeler truck.

Above Signage for Celebrity Golf event and (below) BBQ King Cook off.

Overleaf Rough for typical Bozo's trade advertisement.

Above VIP restaurant booth

Right Bozo's truck BBQ grills at NASCAR events.

SIDE VIEW

CAPE — FLUTTERED BY OUTGOING AIR

TIN ROOF

PIG, FLAT

ARMS FLAT

Opposite Product designs for Howlin' Wolf Whiskey, White Lightnin' Punch Accelerator, Deep Woods Grilling Marinade, and carton design for 3-pack marinades.

STOP IN FOR A BITE
28 ft
MAN EATING SHARK

BOZOS
HOT PIT B.B.Q
SINCE 1923

BEST RIBS @ THE SIGN OF THE FLYING PIG

GRILL

BOZO'S
Hot Pit Bar-B-Q
SINCE 1923
RESTAURANT
AHEAD SOON!

Eye-catching Shark roadside signage; rough sign of the Flying Pig, Bozo's NASCAR racing car.

Left Portrait taken in London, March 2001. **The author Philip Norman interviewed me at my studio in London for the *Sunday Times* magazine. Both of us had worked on the paper in the past, so we reminisced about the good old days. The well-known photographer Gered Mankowitz was to take a picture for the article. Within minutes Gered got the shot – me like Jack Horner sat in the corner, surrounded by the ephemera of my working life. Brilliant.**

Below Cover for J. K. Galbraith's *The Economics of Innocent Fraud.* Pocket Penguin, 2006. **So here I am, forty-one years after I first joined the company, designing a book cover for Penguin as part of their seventieth birthday celebrations and I wonder if all the battles Tony Godwin and I went through back in the sixties with their archaic board have been resolved, i.e. their claim that covers didn't sell books!**

J. K. Galbraith

The Economics of Innocent Fraud

70

The Boy with the Broken Heart began in 2007.
I had this vision of a boy who finds a broken
heart and goes in search of its owner through
a post-Apocalyptic landscape. I wanted to
build small three-dimensional sets and I
mocked up the first one and shot it with a
Leica digital camera. I liked the result and
sometime soon will continue to develop
the project ...

The city had been hurriedly abandoned.
Toxic ash still fell: a grey snow laced with
the cunning of Death.
Moths and bats of enormous size flittered
above the shadowed streets and alleys.
The sky, without stars was permanent
night.
The moon the colour of skulls.
The boy carrying a broken heart,
ventured among the piled debris of past
memories, anxious to find its owner ...

Concept sketch for *The Boy with the
Broken Heart*, 2007.

Solange is an irreverent, imaginative jewelry designer who works in London. She wanted a logo that reflected the lush ornateness of her designs. After the logo was delivered I did further logos for her separate collections: Random (2006), Cosmic (2006) and Stoned (2007).

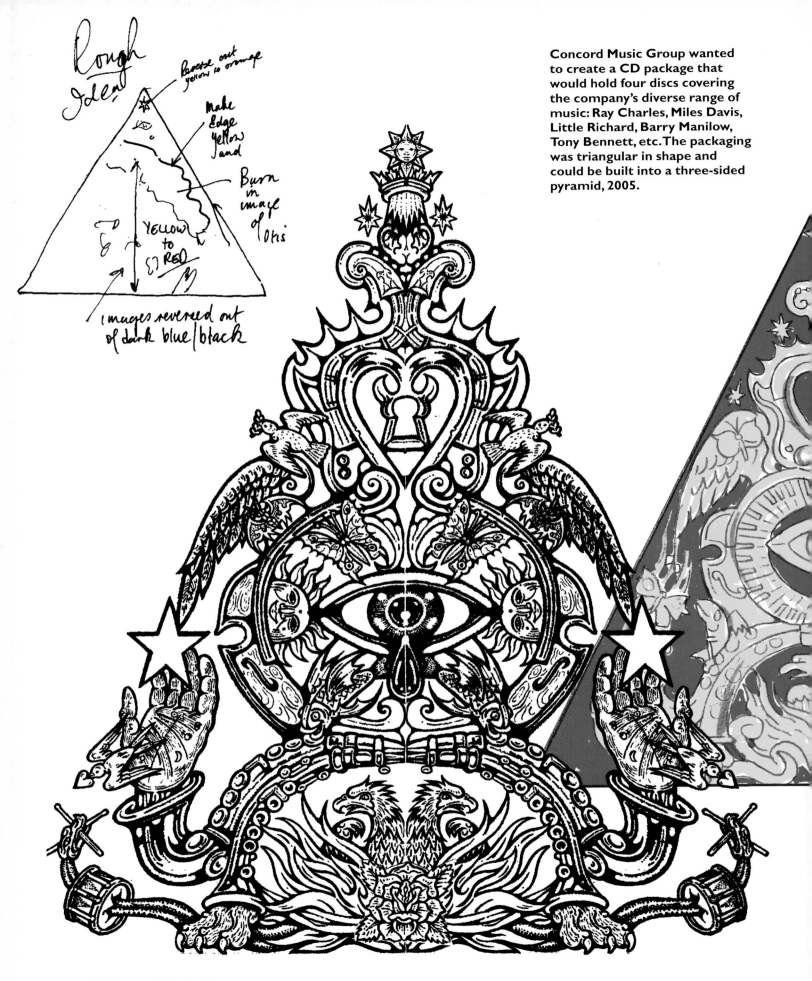

Concord Music Group wanted to create a CD package that would hold four discs covering the company's diverse range of music: Ray Charles, Miles Davis, Little Richard, Barry Manilow, Tony Bennett, etc. The packaging was triangular in shape and could be built into a three-sided pyramid, 2005.

CANCER THE CRAB

RUBY JEWEL.

SWITCH ROUND
PUT IN EYES

MAKE EDGE OF YELLOW MORE PRONOUNCED

ROSY UP CHEEKS

UPSIDEDOWNY TOY

You've got the job — push colors brighter (for plasticy look

INSIDE MOUTH LESS BLACK MORE DARK RED
GO BABY—

Since 2005 there has been an explosion of highly imaginative toy design, mostly from Japan but also in the US. From collectably cute figurines to phantasmorgorical creatures the toys sold through stores like Kidrobot and Toy Tokyo. The toys shown on the spread are ideas in the development stage.

Lil YETI B/W

JUNE 22

21 JULY

AMBITIOUS

TENACIOUS

SENSITIVE

MOODY

POSITIVE

LOYAL

211

Fashion spreads (and overleaf) for the *New York Times* magazine, 29 April 2007. **For four weeks I was up to my neck in photos of dresses, handbags, shoes** and necklaces. The first drawing was the *Ship of Fools* (below), which for **complexity set the tone for all the other illustrations.**

Incubus, *A Crow Left of the Murder* tour,
T-shirt design and elements, 2004.
**I met Mike Einziger, the lead guitarist
of Incubus, through my daughter Lily.
The band was about to start an
American tour and I volunteered
to design a T-shirt.**

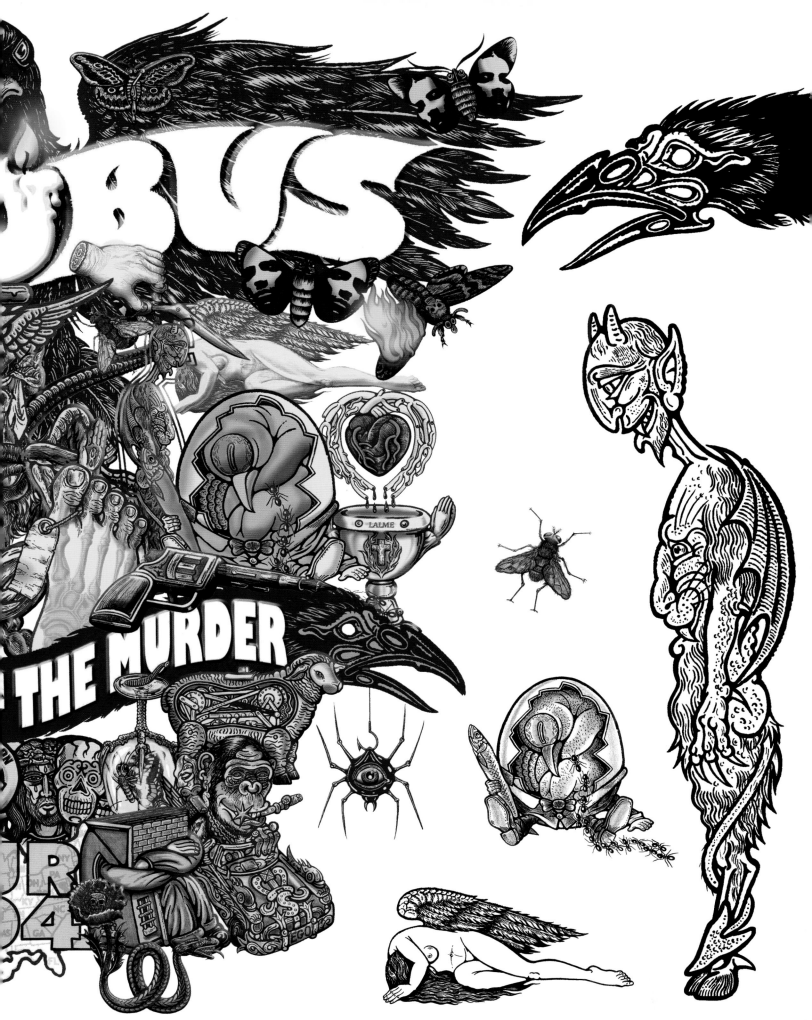

Incubus, *Light Grenades*, CD package,
Epic Records, 2006.
**Brandon Boyd, the lead singer
of Incubus, phoned to ask if I'd design
their next CD. I loved the title *Light
Grenades* and thought of a grenade
with a crystaline structure carved
with symbols of love, peace and
religion. When you pulled the pin and
threw one it burst with showers of
truth and love. Some of the early
versions can be seen opposite. In the
end, using full colour was abandoned
for a simpler approach in two colours.**

Incubus 219

Drawings (sumi pen on vellum) for
Light Grenades lyrics booklet, 2006.
Above 'Rogues'.
Left 'Earth to Bella'.
Right 'Paper Shoes'.

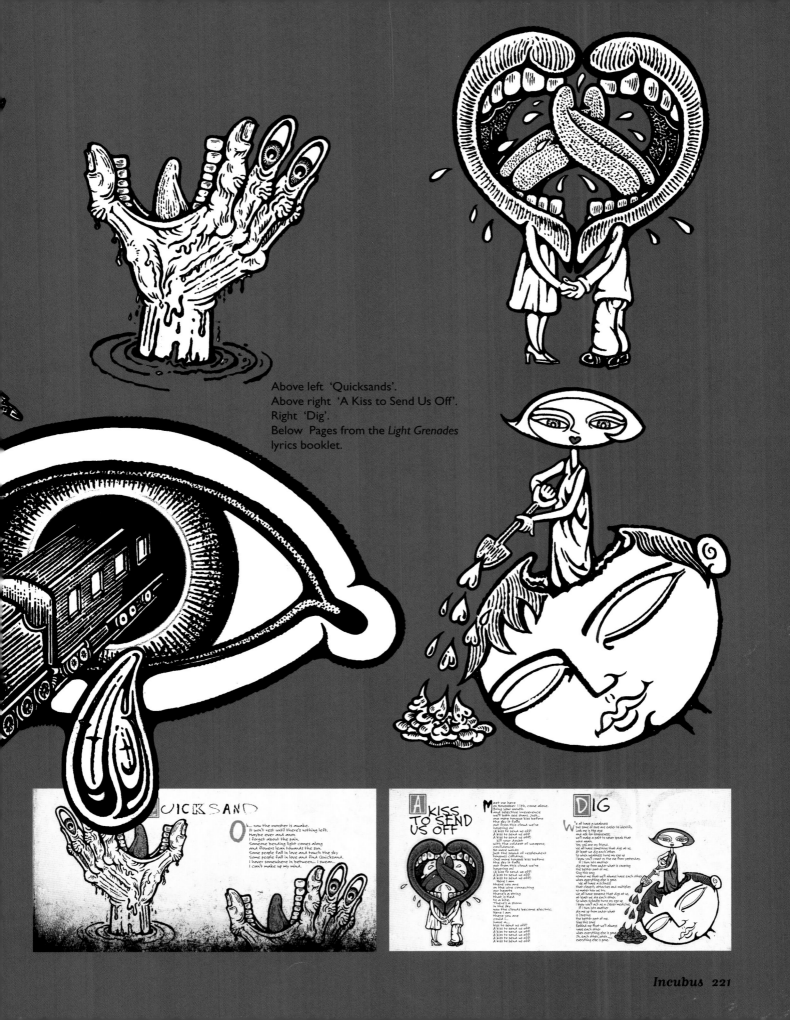

Above left 'Quicksands'.
Above right 'A Kiss to Send Us Off'.
Right 'Dig'.
Below Pages from the *Light Grenades* lyrics booklet.

Running around page 'Light Grenades' video storyboard, 2007.

I presented this to Incubus for an animated video for the song 'Light Grenades'. The video didn't get made.

Below left 'Anna-Molly' CD cover. Opposite centre Finished artwork, Epic Records, 2006.

'Anna-Molly' (perhaps a pun on anomaly) was a single issued some weeks before the *Light Grenades* CD.

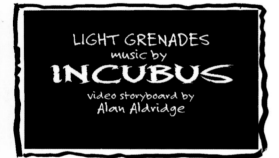

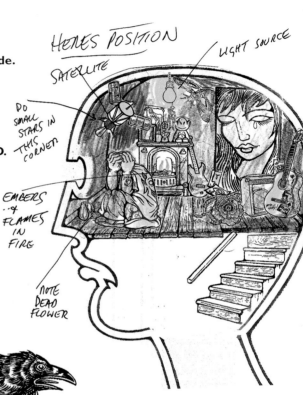

HENES POSITION
LIGHT SOURCE
SATELLITE
DO SMALL STARS IN THIS CORNET
EMBERS & FLAMES IN FIRE
NOTE DEAD FLOWER

LIGHT GRENADES
music by
INCUBUS
video storyboard by
Alan Aldridge

ROUGH WHITE BORDED

ANNA-MOLLY

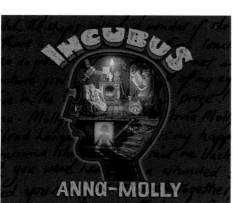

DONE THIS IS STAIRWELL SHADOW OF GIRL LEAVING GOING DOWNSTAIRS

FOR POSITION

IMAGE SHOULD BE SOFT AND DOORWAY

SHADOW WOULD BE ON STAIRS

DONT MAKE SHADOW BLACK ITS GREY AND SHOULD BE ABLE TO READ GRAFITI

DEATH IS GLORY!

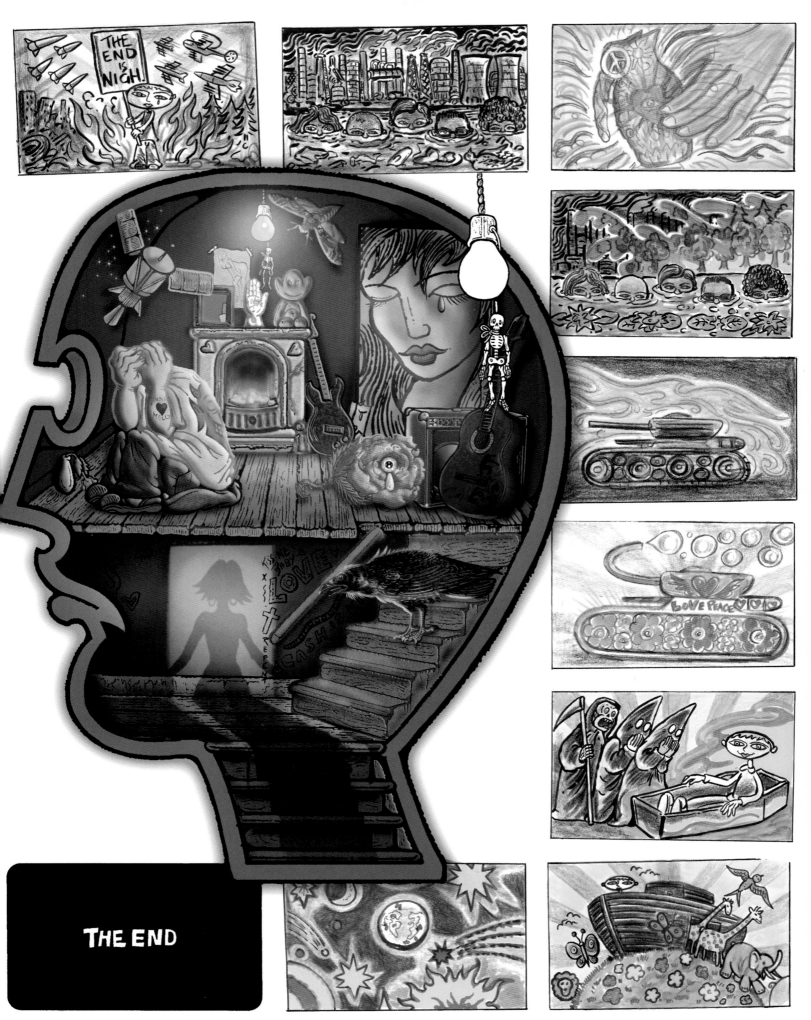

THE END

A B C D E } Take from photo and strip in

POSITION IN HOLE.

BIRDY IN BOTH EYES OF TREE. RED KEYLINE, YELLOW FEATHERS

TREE

MODEL UNDER ARMS & FINGERS

BIRD
MORE MODE
BLUSH YELLO
TO MAKE E
MORE CLEA

MAKE WIN
FEATHER
RED

← RED

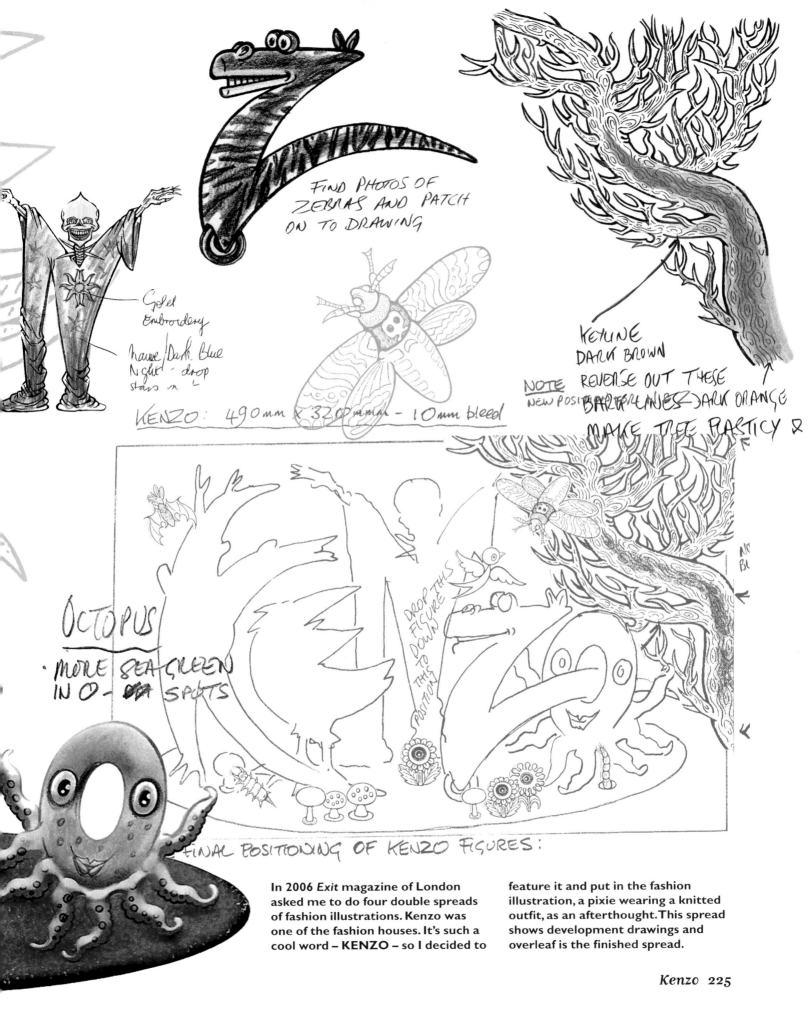

FIND PHOTOS OF ZEBRAS AND PATCH ON TO DRAWING

Gold Embroidery

Mauve/Dark Blue Night - deep stars in

KENZO: 490mm x 320mm - 10mm bleed

KEYLINE DARK BROWN

NOTE REVERSE OUT THESE BAR LINES DARK ORANGE
NEW POSITION

MAKE TREE PLASTICY &

OCTOPUS

• MORE SEA GREEN IN O - SPOTS

DROP THIS FIGURE DOWN TO THIS POSITION

FINAL POSITIONING OF KENZO FIGURES:

In 2006 *Exit* magazine of London asked me to do four double spreads of fashion illustrations. Kenzo was one of the fashion houses. It's such a cool word – **KENZO** – so I decided to feature it and put in the fashion illustration, a pixie wearing a knitted outfit, as an afterthought. This spread shows development drawings and overleaf is the finished spread.

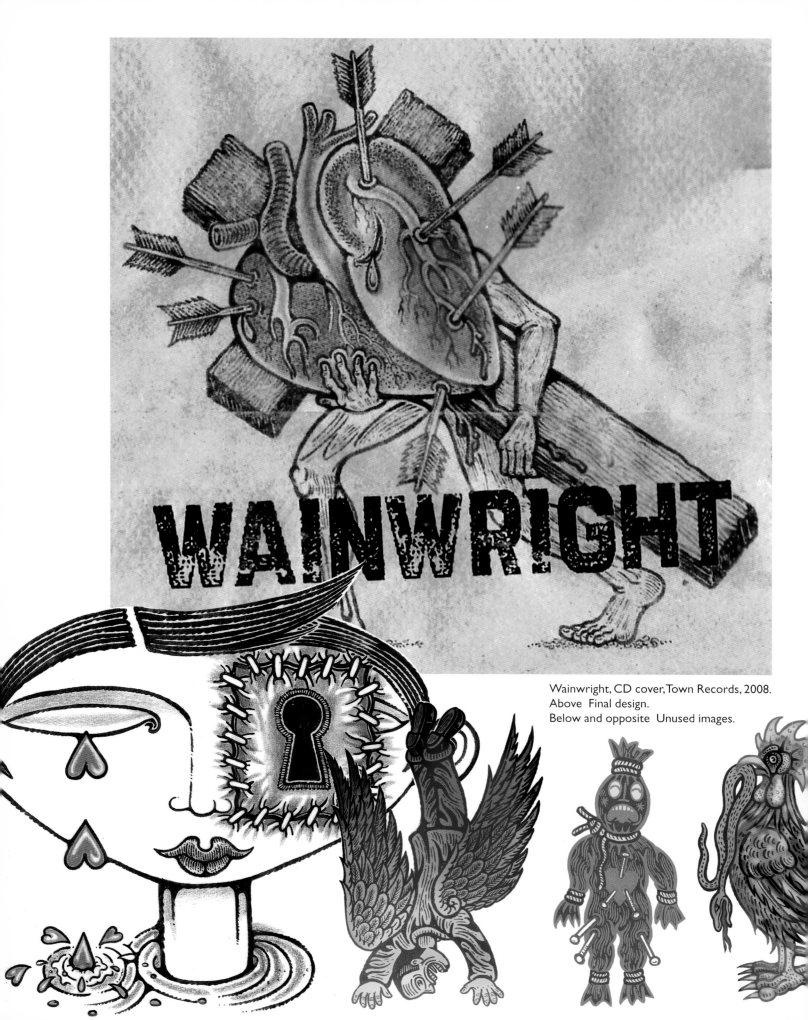

Wainwright, CD cover, Town Records, 2008.
Above Final design.
Below and opposite Unused images.

Above *Paranoia*, 2006. Unpublished drawing.

The *New York Times* magazine wanted a portrait of me to accompany the fashion spreads I did for them (see pp. 212–15). My first choice as photographer was my son Miles and luckily he was coming to Los Angeles for a fashion assignment. At my shoot, Miles jokingly said I had to do as I was told, not to comment on anything and not to make any creative suggestions. *Fait accompli.* Great photo. 2007.

What next? I've designed a wine label for Green Lion Wines, am about to launch Alan Aldridge Inc. – a merchandising/licensing company to exploit all the images I've created over the years – have ideas for new books, a film treatment or two, and who knows what's hovering around the corner?

I'd developed a great movie idea, *Nothing is Real*, an animated fantasy about John Lennon's childhood, the reality of his chaotic home life countered by the magical world of make-believe he created. I obtained Yoko's approval to show it around Hollywood. I got Klasky Csupo, a highly creative independent animation house (*Rugrats*, *Wild Thornberrys*, *The Simpsons*), on board as production company. There were endless story meetings, rewrites and re-drawing of the characters until the film had moved away from my initial vision. They shipped a beautiful presentation kit to Yoko, but she didn't like it. The project reverted to me. It'll happen one of these days.

Opposite Illustration for proposed animated film, *Nothing is Real*, 2008.
The story is about John Lennon's childhood and this image depicts the night he was born, 9 October 1940, during an air raid on Liverpool.

Below 'The Death of Humpty Dumpty', from *Trippy Tales*, 2008.

Overleaf *Trippy Tales*, cover artwork and elements, 2008.

Trippy Tales (or How Far Down the Rabbit Hole Do You Want To Fall?) **is a work in progress and is going to be a book of bizarre short stories done in much the same way I did** *Butterfly Ball*. **I'm creating twelve drawings and will write stories for each one. Again, like** *Butterfly Ball*, **I've done the cover artwork first. I'll publish the book as a limited edition.**

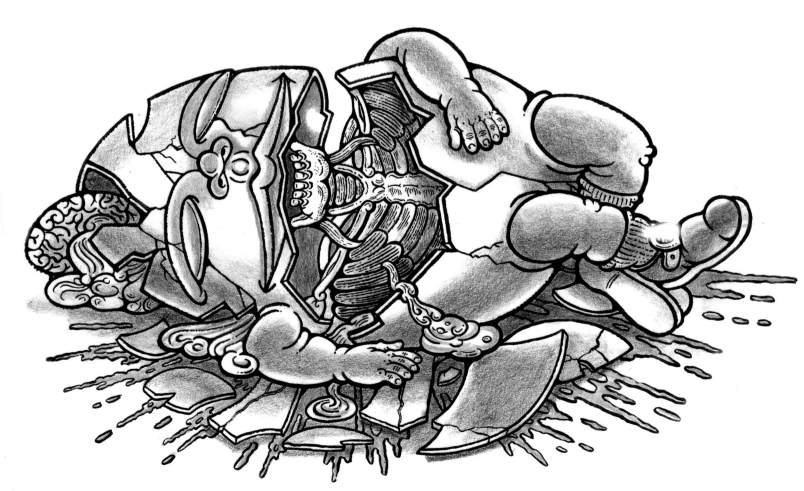

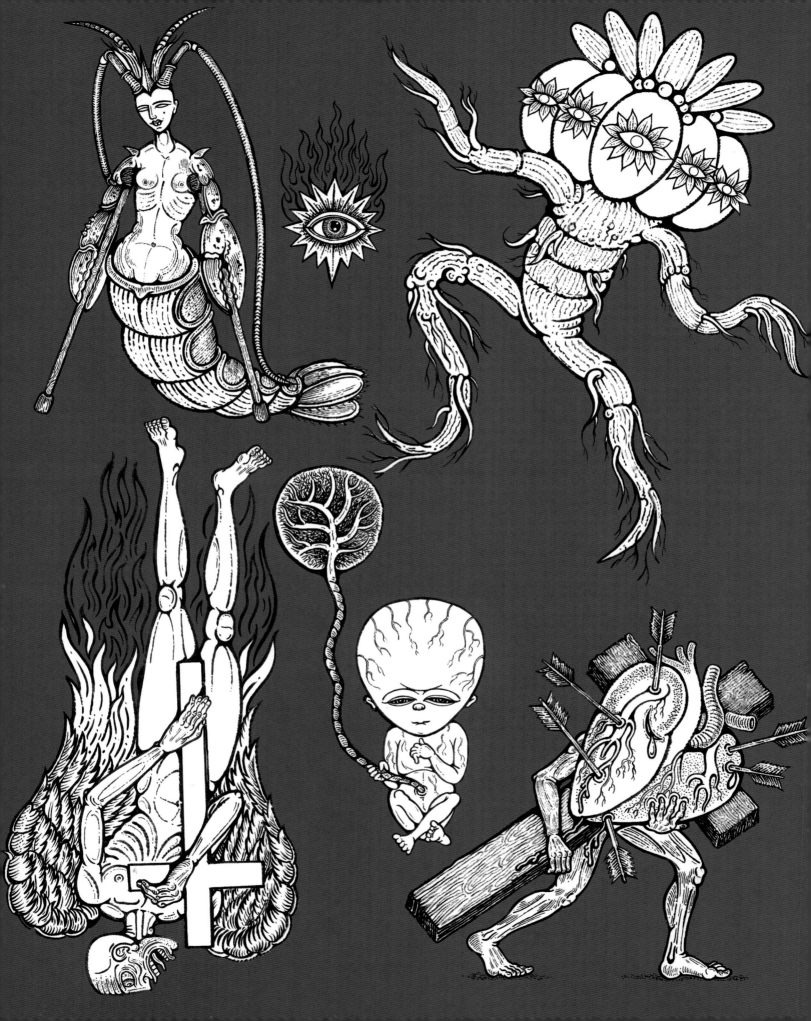

L

M

N

O

P

R

Q

R

S

**To all my amazing children
and grandchildren.
And their beautiful mothers.**

Acknowledgments

A huge thank you to all those people I have
worked with who helped to fill the pages
of this book over the years and especially
to the following: Harry Willock, good friend,
who worked in the trenches with me from
1965 to 1985 and finally again in 1995 with
the House of Blues logo; Dave Fleming
who started working with me on the
House of Blues Atlanta adventure in 1996
and continues his Mac-monkey wizardry;
and Lanning Aldrich and Anthony Jayes for
wise counsel and good friendship. Also a big
thank you to Phil Baines, Julia MacKenzie
and all the staff at Thames & Hudson who
put this book together.

Credits

p. 11   Courtesy Laurie Wierzbicki
p. 13   Photographs by John Deakin
p. 45   Copyright Snowdon
pp. 48–49   Photographs by Brian Duffy
p. 51   The Sean O'Mahony Collection
pp. 74–75   Photographs by Roger Phillips
p. 80   Courtesy Burton Silverman,
   Silverman Studios Inc.
p. 81   Photograph by Leonard Burt/Central
   Press/Getty Images
p. 82 bottom right   Getty Images
p. 83 top right   Photograph by Neil Libbert.
   Courtesy Michael Hoppen Gallery
p. 131 top   Photograph by Paul Finch
p. 169 top right   *Rolling Stone*® is a
   registered trademark of Rolling Stone
   LLC. All Rights Reserved. *Rolling Stone*
   materials used by permission
p. 202   Photograph by Gered Mankowitz.
   Copyright BOWSTIR Ltd 2008/
   mankowitz.com
p. 230   Photograph by Miles Aldridge
Additional material loaned by Phil Baines,
   Central Saint Martins College of Art &
   Design, Catherine Dixon and David
   Pearson

First published in the United Kingdom
in 2008 by Thames & Hudson Ltd,
181A High Holborn, London WC1V 7QX

www.thamesandhudson.com

British Library Cataloguing-in-Publication
Data
A catalogue record for this book is available
from the British Library

ISBN 978-0-500-09342-9

Designed by Phil Baines
Layout by Phil Baines & Max Ackermann,
assisted by Ipek Altunmaral
Copystand photography by Max Ackermann

Printed and bound in China by
SNP Leefung Printers Ltd

Page 1   Animation idea for home page
www.alanaldridge.net

Right   Final illustration from
The Peacock Party, 1979.